Lee Marks is the CEO of UK based company Break the Silence UK, and the author on the subject of domestic abuse. Having worked in this field for a number of years and being a survivor of abuse himself, Lee has a passion to share his knowledge and raise awareness through books and training courses. His work in this field saw him become a finalist in the category of Activist of the Year at the 2020 Men and Boys Awards.

My darling wife, Clare, for her unwavering support throughout the development of this book.

My children, Jennifer and Harrison, for their understanding when development kept me busy for whole weekends.

Josh Munro for his collaboration on some of the chapters in the book and for his honest appraisal of the content.

All the victims and survivors of abuse, whose experiences have helped to shape the pages of this book.

Lee Marks

Break the Silence – A Support Guide for Male Victims of Domestic Abuse

AUSTIN MACAULEY PUBLISHERS™

LONDON • CAMBRIDGE • NEW YORK • SHARJAH

A CIP catalogue record for this title is available from the British Library.

ISBN 9781398434905 (Paperback)
ISBN 9781398434912 (ePub e-book)

www.austinmacauley.com

First Published 2021
Austin Macauley Publishers Ltd®
1 Canada Square
Canary Wharf
London
E14 5AA

Well, that brings me to the end of this journey, the journey of sharing what I have learnt with you as it has been shared with me. I hope that for those of you that are yourselves survivors of abuse, some of what you have read about in these pages may have helped you in some way to understand and come to terms with what you have been through. For those of you, as with some of the men I've come to know and whom I am proud to call friends that still fight for the rights to see and have contact with their children, I hope that the information in that section I have provided in these covers may be invaluable to you.

To those of you that were given this book by a loved one or picked it up out of interest or curiosity and have taken the time to read what is held within these pages, maybe because you yourself just felt that something wasn't right in your relationship or maybe you already knew that you were a victim of abuse, I hope that some of the content that you have read has opened your eyes to more of the behaviours that you are experiencing, that maybe you didn't think of as abusive. But let me reiterate something with you as I shared in the book, this is normal with the majority of male victims of abuse. The majority of the men that I have supported over the years have been through the same journey of discovery that you may have just been on, that more of their partners' behaviours were abusive and about power and control than they recognised. What is important now is that you recognise this now and that you realise that you are not alone, that there are options open to you. There are many agencies out there that can and will listen when you are ready to talk about what you are or have experienced.

Even though this book is solely aimed at male victims of abuse, I would also like to address family members that I know will have picked this up and read through this book to gain more of an insight into what their loved ones may have suffered or are currently going through. Hopefully, what you read within these pages has given you an understanding of some of the issues they may have had or are at this moment suffering and that insight has given you some clarity in the situation. The most important advice I can give you is to be there, never give up hope as one day, when that time comes, they will need your help but will be too scared or too ashamed to ask you for it. But to just let them know you are there when they need it, just to listen and not judge, is the biggest thing you can do for them.

I have a lot of people that I would like to thank for their help not only in writing of this book but for their guidance in my learning and understanding around the issues of domestic abuse. Firstly, I want to thank my wife Clare and my children Jennifer and Harrison for their patience and support whilst I have been putting this together, the late nights working after doing my day job and the endless supply of coffee and chocolate that I have been provided. Clare, you have been my rock not just through this process but in life generally and especially when I was working in the domestic abuse field as at times, the experiences I shared were not easy but you were there, without asking questions. You have taught me the practical experience of what a healthy relationship is, even if we do have our differences from time to time, so thank you from the bottom of my heart.

I would also like to thank members of my family without naming names; we've been through some really rough times together over the years but come out fighting. I am so amazingly proud of all of you and to be able to stand by your side and say I'm your brother. And to my mum who has always been there, even at times when she has had her own problems that she has faced. I want to send her a small message which I hope she will understand after reading this book. See Mum, look at where I am now, look at all the people my experiences have helped. What happened in the past was never your fault and it's time to let that go.

A massive thank you must go to my team at Break the Silence UK, Amy and Josh. Amy you were a great sounding board as I wrote the first draft, encouraging me to look at different angles as the book came together. I thank you for broadening my horizon on this subject. And Josh, who because of his background with domestic abuse services and working with male victims, became my trusted advisor and collaborator in this project. You have had a major role in helping shape this book and all the information it holds, even to the extent of adding information I wasn't aware of! It's funny that we only met face to face for the first time a few years ago, but due to our work in this field our paths have been very close for a number of years. Thank you so much for what you have done, you've been an immense help with this project and I look forward to collaborating with you both on the next project.

I would like to thank my friend and mentor when it comes to the development of my knowledge of domestic abuse, Jack Webb, who educated me around a lot of the issues that I knew nothing about and provided me with support with some of my own personal demons from previous relationships. Without you, mate, I'd probably would have never ventured into this type of support field and not developed massively as a person. Bringing me in to work alongside you has changed my life in so many ways because of how passionate I have become about this topic and most importantly, it has brought me to this point where I have written this book! Your guidance around the differences between someone using power and control and someone being supportive opened my eyes to a lot of things that I had never considered.

It would be amiss of me not to thank some of my other colleagues from when I worked in the domestic abuse service that had a massive impact on the service users that they worked with and in supporting me through the difficult times. Firstly, Paula Kay, my mentor from the women's service who was always there to bounce thoughts off when the times arose that I supported female victims and to correct me when I over thought things (which was quite often). My years working in the domestic abuse team in Worcestershire bought me into contact with so many fantastic workers that always gave their all to their service users, workers like my good friends Sam Skilbeck and Agnes Czapla.

Outside of the service, I do have to say a massive thank you to Martin Lakeman who was the lead on all things domestic abuse within my area. On a number of occasions, he gave me the opportunity to speak out for male victims and address a number of professionals from all different backgrounds within the Worcestershire Domestic Abuse Forum Day events. Martin I would also like to thank you from the bottom of my heart for your guidance and support around the personal issues that have affected my family.

Coming to the here and now, and the network of professionals that I am privileged to share time with and work alongside. Experts in their field, such as Mark Brooks OBE of Mankind Initiative and the Men and Boys Coalition, Sally-Anne Burris of Split the Difference CIC, and the massively inspirational Robert Wells of Domestic Abuse Business Support

Ltd. Their continued support for what we have, and continue to try to achieve, has kept us going. A special mention must also go to all the amazing people involved with the Paul Lavelle Foundation. Paul was a victim who lost his life and the foundation was started in his memory. I have been fortunate to share in part of this journey and to observe them going from strength to strength. Two moments shared with you stick with me. Meeting Paul's mum Barbara and having the chance to speak to her was a very emotional moment for me personally, and being in Bristol as your group of cyclists came around the corner to meet me, whilst on your Lands' End to John O'Groats ride raising awareness of male victims of abuse. Seeing the effort you were going through in memory of Paul has been a motivator for me and your friendship is beyond words.

But the biggest thank you of all has to go to the victims and survivors of abuse that I have had the pleasure of knowing and working with. Thank you for sharing your personal experiences and journeys with me, I am truly humbled by your trust and belief in the support I provided and for what you have included me in. You have all shown massive amounts of strength and courage in dealing with what you have and you genuinely are all truly amazing people. To those of you that I unfortunately no longer have contact with, I hope beyond all hopes that you have gone on to have happy lives and come to know peace over what has happened to you.

Finally, thank you once again to all of you that have purchased this book and gone on this journey with me. We've looked at domestic abuse in general, ventured through the types of abuse exploring the tactics used and practical advice to help move forward. I just live in the hope of a day when we manage to educate everyone enough to significantly reduce the number of victims, if not eradicate this social issue. But until then, we keep doing what we do.

www.breakthesilenceuk.co.uk

Table of Contents

Foreword

It has taken me some time with the help of my collaborator Josh, to pull together all the resources and information that I needed to complete this book, as well as a lot of soul searching. I remember thinking to myself *"Is putting all this knowledge I have out there the right thing to do?"* As the old phrase goes, "knowledge is power" and could I be putting this information into the wrong hands. Many nights I mulled this over, holding many conversations with both Josh and Amy from my team at Break the Silence UK. But in the end, it came down to the fact that ultimately, domestic abuse affects us all in so many different ways and most people have experienced it themselves, or had a family member or friend go through abuse and have shared in their experiences.

Despite what some believe, men too can be victims of domestic abuse and the result of what they experience, although in some ways different, are just as bad as those suffered by female victims. Statistics say that an estimated 757,000 men experienced domestic abuse in 2019-2020 which is an astronomical number. To put it in a way that more people can relate to they say 1 in 6 men suffer abuse, so take a rugby union side with 15 players and 7 or 8 substitutes, 3 of that side statistically suffer from abuse. My personal belief is that this is a conservative guess, the word estimate is just that and the actual figure would be a lot higher than this if we actually lived in a society where men could come forward so that we knew of more incidents. From experience, a lot of the men that I have worked with have said that before they really understood what it was, the behaviours they faced from their partners on an almost daily occurrence, may not have felt right to them but it became the "norm", and they would never have considered to label these behaviours as domestic abuse. It could be very moving to see them generally feel shocked when the realisation sets in of the situations they were in.

When domestic abuse is talked about, it is predominantly done in regards to a female victim and a male perpetrator. Society as a whole does seem more accepting of the female victim and open to talk about it, maybe due to the publicity around the feminist movement and their campaign for equality for women. The government themselves have the strategy to end violence towards women and girls 2016 to 2020, which may I just say that I agree with and support 100%. But what about the male and LGBTQ victims? Do we see just as many stories in the press speaking about them and the risks that they face? Has the government created a strategy to end violence towards either of these groups? Not at this moment they have not, they have put slightly more financially into a small selection of male services but a strategy is something that needs to be explored as the risks and dangers to men are also very real. The option for the government to take a real stance was there whilst gathering evidence for the landmark Domestic Abuse Bill, but unfortunately male services only received a little time and provided less than 5% of the evidence given.

Over the years, I have had the experience of working with both male and female survivors of abuse both when I was working directly within domestic abuse services, and others I have met within my various day to day jobs. I have become good friends with men who have suffered severely with their mental health, men who have turned to substances as the only way to cope with their situations and on numerous occasions, men who have cried all the way through the time we have spent together in support sessions because the reactions they would receive from "society" prevents them from doing so in the outside world. Then there are the few cases of the men who have felt that the situations they were in left them with no other option but to take their own lives as they saw no other way out. Statistics that are out there in mainstream records currently show that suicide is the biggest killer of men under the age of 49 in the UK, one of the leading causes of death in males aged 16 to 24 and in males in the LGBT community. I was once asked my opinion during a radio interview on how many of those suicides could have been as a result of these men being victims of domestic abuse. The only answer that can be given to that is unfortunately we will never know, however, it is not beyond the realms of possibility with what is seen as the distinct lack of services available to male victims to access, how males perceive that they will be viewed by those they disclose to, society and their viewpoints in general and for some, as I have already alluded to, quite simply a lack of understanding of the fact that what they are suffering is abuse.

As with the majority of the men I worked with, there will be many more out there that aren't included within the statistics that are victims of abuse. For some of those, their thinking, again like so many others, may be that it is just a bad patch and that it would get better. I can't remember the times I have been told that men have reasoned with themselves by telling themselves just that.

For me, my own knowledge only began to develop when I was invited to help a colleague to co-facilitating a programme designed to aid male victims of abuse called Rejuvenate (which led into my working with male victims of domestic abuse across Worcestershire). The aim of the programme was to support male victims to accept and come to terms with what they had been living with and to be able to recognise the behaviours that they faced for just what they were. It was then that I realised the extent of just how much men were suffering. For some, it was just emotional but for others it got much worse with physical and even sexual abuse. But no matter what type of abuse and tactics that were used, abuse is abuse and there is no place for it in modern society.

What with my personal experiences and those of another family member that I was once so very close to, and having spent many years working full-time supporting male victims of domestic abuse, and throughout its development, the decision to write this book became easy the more I reflected on the material. I felt compelled to continue with my work and further the support that I have already offered to many by sharing the knowledge that I have learned and experiences I have shared within these pages. We will explore the difficulties and risks considered by victims when it comes to making decisions on if to flee abusive home life or to stay in the relationship, to understand what has happened to them and experience what some have gone through, hopefully some of this will also help you.

This book is predominantly aimed at male victims of abuse and professionals that come into contact with them. On the whole, I do refer to the perpetrator as a she, but I also acknowledge that men in same-sex relationships can also be victims of abuse. With that in mind, my team has spent some dedicated time pulling together a section to look at same-sex relationships and the abuse that can be suffered on top of all the other abuse identified.

Hopefully what can be found within these pages can provide a great source of guidance to more than just the victims, but also to their friends and families so as they too can understand what it is their son, brother, uncle, friend is going through and to try and understand why they may be behaving in the way that they are. For you, I hope this book can give some clarity and understanding of their situations for when the time hopefully comes that they do seek help.

My experiences have massively shaped the information that is held within this book, I will talk openly about some of my experiences with other agencies and about some of the situations men that I know have found themselves in. The aim of this book is to help other men who are out there to not only gain an understanding of what is happening to them but to realise that they are not as alone as they may feel. With all I will cover, I hope everyone reading will be able to see that abuse is abuse, regardless of gender, and to explore the options that are open to victims, including keeping themselves safe and their legal options.

The experiences I have shared have given me a real passion to try and help men who have suffered years of torment to find understanding and be able to move on and rebuild their own lives. It has led to the creation of our company Break the Silence UK with the aim to support all victims of domestic abuse, regardless of gender. All I can say is, nobody deserves to live in fear, and hopefully what I share in these pages can help some to move forward and seek help that is on offer.

Lee Marks

Chapter One
Domestic Abuse – What Is It?

So just what is domestic abuse? This is the big question. Formally it was referred to as domestic violence, for some it still is. But it became more apparent that over the years it was so much more than just intimate partner violence. The government define domestic abuse as:

Any incident or pattern of incidents of controlling, coercive or threatening behaviour, violence or abuse between those aged 16 or over who are or have been intimate partners or family members regardless of gender or sexuality. This can encompass but is not limited to the following types of abuse:

- Psychological
- Physical
- Sexual
- Financial
- Emotional

This definition, which is not a legal definition, includes so-called "honour" based violence, female genital mutilation

(FGM) and forced marriage, and is clear that victims are not confined to one gender or ethnic group.

Quite straight forward in terms of an explanation, don't you think? But the fact of the matter is that for many men, they do not see the link between these categories of abuse and the behaviours that they are facing themselves by their partners or family members in everyday life. Many just don't see domestic abuse as an issue that effects men. Why would this be? Could it be the minimal amount of publicity through various media platforms relating to male victims and only usually portraying female victims?

I have also asked a number of professionals that I know, how confident they are that they could define what controlling and coercive behaviour looks like, and most struggle to do so. So here it is, our government defines it:

- Coercive behaviour is an act or pattern of assaults, threats, humiliation and intimidation or other abuse that is used to harm, punish or frighten their victim.
- Controlling behaviour is a range of acts designed to make a person subordinate and/or dependent by isolating them from sources of support, exploiting their resources and capacities for personal gain, depriving them of the means needed for independence, resistance and escape through regulating their everyday behaviour.

One of the males that I once worked with described coercive control as living the life of a hostage as they never know from one day to the next what would happen, the only thing certain was the fear that they felt for that unknown. Fear is a central component to coercive control; it can feel like a world of constantly moving goal-posts and commonly described as living a life of walking on eggshells.

The government definition in itself makes things just a little clearer but throughout this book, we will go a little deeper in looking at the types of behaviours that could be displayed and how these constitute abuse.

One of the most important things for male victims to realise is that you are not alone; there are thousands if not millions of other men that are either in or have been in a similar position to you. And being a victim isn't just restricted to certain walks of life or age groups, I myself have worked with all sorts of people of all ages. I have worked with men who are unemployed yes, but I have also worked with professional men, accountants, sports men, firemen, authors, men from all walks of life. And most had one thing in common, those around them, those that probably saw them on a daily basis, their neighbours and work colleagues, sometimes family members (if they were still in contact) did not know that anything wrong was going on within the relationship.

To emphasise this a little further with you, I thought I would share some figures relating to male victims of abuse from a number of surveys taken over the last few years:

- 15% of men aged 16 to 59 in the UK have experienced some form of domestic abuse since the age of 16, which is the equivalent to an estimated 2.4 million male victims of domestic abuse.
- 4.3% of men in the UK have experienced domestic abuse in the last 12 months. This is only 3.2% lower

than that reported by females which is the lowest difference since 2005. This only goes to show that the difference in numbers between male and female victims is closing.

- In 2016/2017, 13 men were killed by their partner or former partner. That equates to slightly over 1 per month. This number is down from 20 in 2015/2016 which is an amazing reduction but 13 men per year is still 13 too many.

Why don't male victims report?

"If it's that bad, why don't they just leave?" This seems to be the universal question asked about any victim of abuse, be they male or female, by people that don't have an understanding of domestic abuse and what it does to the individual. It seems an easy response, doesn't it? I have also lectured on male victims of abuse and openly had other males within the room say "if that was me, she'd get the back of my hand and that would be that." Violence resolved with violence; paints a beautiful view of the world, don't you think? Problem is that there are a number of men that are currently in prison or have served sentences for reaching breaking point and retaliating to ongoing and persistent abuse and that one time has resulted in the perpetrator calling the police, the tables being turned and the victim being labelled a perpetrator of abuse.

So, what explanation can there be to why men struggle to just walk away? In most cases men are physically stronger so how can these women stop them from leaving? What is it that keeps them held within the relationship? The truth is there isn't one universal reason why, there is an abundance of reasons why men don't just walk away. The most common reason that I have come across and still come across being that they are concerned about leaving their children. Well surely, if things were that bad, they would take the children with them? If only it was that easy. It is a sad fact but in the majority of cases where there are children involved, residency of the children is awarded to the mother. This is a major hold that a female perpetrator would have over their male victim and the fear that they will never see their children again is very real. But not only this, for a large number of men, they would not question that their partner is a good mother despite all that she is putting them through and cannot live with the thought of taking the children from their mother. However, the children do need to be considered here, which will be covered later on within this book because the abuse does have a profound effect on them too.

There are four other main reasons reported by men why they don't just leave their partners. Firstly, they still love them and hope that they can change. They've had good times and hope that this is just a bump in the road that together they can overcome, and the perpetrator can be extremely convincing of this fact. If the couple is married, there is also still a common-held belief that marriage is for life and that can be a reason in itself to remain in the relationship. Look at Christianity, the words used are that it is a lifelong contract between partners and that it is for "as long as you both shall live". In the eyes of the Roman Catholic Church, divorce is forbidden and as such partners should try to resolve their differences. They can still apply for a civil divorce but will be unable to remarry in the eyes of the church. Along a similar line, within the black,

Asian and ethnic minority communities, you have the situations of arranged marriages. For a male victim who is part of an arranged marriage, it isn't as simple as just religion, as to leave this union also means for many being shunned by their family, their friends and the entire community.

Another reason that is quite common that keeps a male within an abusive relationship is the lack of resources available for them to leave. This includes money (which we will talk about later in economic abuse) and to even have somewhere to go. Many have lost contact with family members so are in a position that they feel they do not have anyone that they could even approach to ask for help. Granted there are safe houses and refuges across the UK, but it is unlikely that a male will be able to access one of these. In the UK alone, there are 3,798 bed spaces in refuge and safe house accommodation, 175 of these beds are accessible for men. That is, a figure of 4.5% of the beds can be accessed by men. What is not commonly known is that only about 40 of these beds are reserved solely for male use, the others can and usually are accessed by female victims which means just over 1% of the bed space is available to be accessed solely by men. However, all is not lost. A male victim of abuse can approach a local authority for help with emergency accommodation under Housing Act 1996 and Homelessness Act of 2002. They would have to be considered in exactly the same way as a female victim would be, however reluctant they may be to do so.

On a par with this as a reason is that of embarrassment, they feel embarrassed to talk about what has happened to them due to what people may think of them. Things have gotten better but it does still happen that people are judged by society for what happens to them. Take for example a situation in which a top model/actress (I use the word actress in the loosest possible term) openly wrote in her autobiography about punching two of her ex-boyfriends in the face due to what can only be described as jealousy. Both occasions were on nights out in front of a number of other people and both sadly went unreported. But that is hardly surprising, especially if you factor into this that one was an action film star and the other a professional rugby player, any report that they were victims of abuse and were physically assaulted wouldn't really support their image and therefore their careers, would it? What I find even more distressing than this is the perpetrator's response to what it was that she had done. When challenged on her behaviour, this was what she had to say, "I'm not going to do that in the future, I'm just going to pick more wisely the men I be with.". Really? No apology to them for what she had done, it's unacceptable, just "I'll be more careful with who I date in the future", putting the blame solely on her victims, making it their fault or victim blaming, to use the correct terminology. This was then followed up with another blinding quote a day later as a result of the outcry for what she had said. This was a direct quote: "These are big men I'm going out with; I mean look at me, I'm not going to do them any damage!" So, because they are big men it excuses this type of behaviour, does it? I'm not sure which of these quotes I find more insulting.

The final two reasons that are common with male victims are that they are concerned about what their perpetrator will do. Not just to them as the victim but actual harm to themselves as a large number of victims have reported that their perpetrator has apologised and then threatened to kill themselves if their partner leaves following an "outburst". Take abuse out of the equation, how many people would want another's death on their conscience? Not many, I imagine, if any at all. Now imagine how that dynamic must feel to somebody that is in a vulnerable position, as the victim is. On top of this common situation, there is constant worry of what the perpetrator would do to them if they caught them trying to leave, if they found out where they were, should they successfully get away and who else this may put in danger (family, friends, co-workers).

As I said, these are only the most common reasons that I have come across. But this is not a definitive list as for each person, their reasons for remaining are personal only to them. There are many, many reasons why someone would stay in an abusive relationship, some that we may never understand unless we were to find ourselves in that same position and I hope that those that haven't, never will.

Chapter Two
May I Introduce You to
the Cycle of Abuse?

You may be looking at the title of this chapter and thinking what the hell is that? Despite the thoughts of some professionals in the field, the cycle of abuse is a real thing and it gives a detailed overview of what someone within an abusive relationship will be going through.

The cycle of abuse was developed in the 1970s by American psychologist Lenore Walker to explain patterns of behaviour within an abusive relationship. The idea was originally based on female victims but it became clear that male victims and same-sex victims also would go through the same cycle of abuse. So, what does the cycle of abuse look like? It looks like this:

- Tension building
- Incident
- Reconciliation
- Calm

The cycle of abuse is described as having four parts or phases to it, these being tension building, incident, reconciliation (or honeymoon period) and calm. The cycle usually always follows this order time after time, sometimes over 100 times, until the cycle is broken usually by the victim becoming a survivor and leaving the relationship. The cycle itself can vary in the time it takes to go through; for most of the survivors I have worked with, they would describe it as taking months if not longer in the initial stages of the relationship but the longer they were together, the more frequent the incidents became within smaller periods of time, sometimes down to days between outburst.

So, let's start by looking at each of the stages individually.

Tension Building:

This is when the stress and strain in the relationship starts to build up leading to an incident. This can be over many different things; a disagreement over the children, family conflict, something as simple as a basic misunderstanding. During this period the perpetrator will feel that they are being ignored, can become annoyed and this leads them to believe that they have been wronged in some way. They may become quite passive aggressive at this point and one noticeable feature is that their communication becomes quite poor.

It is during this phase that a perpetrator will try to pick fights or cause arguments with their victim, they may become jealous or possessive and they may start to criticise their victim over anything and everything that they do. This behaviour will usually lead on to them making some form of threat, either verbal or physical, and in general their behaviour will become very unpredictable.

Victims that have been through the cycle a few times generally will recognise this behaviour and know that their reactions could trigger an abusive response. Because of this, they will try to appease the perpetrator by becoming compliant. Underneath all of this though, they will be feeling a degree of fear and anxiety of what they know is coming and generally feel like they are walking on eggshells. In some cases, I have had survivors who had been through this cycle many times over the years report how they would provoke their perpetrator to get the incident over with. Obviously, this comes with a whole range of risks and dangers on their own and goes against the concept of safety planning that is the usual fundamental part of support. The result of this action did bring the incident to a head sooner than it may have without provocation, but the physical abuse was worse in most cases as the perpetrator became angry that they weren't in control of the situation.

Incident:

This phase is characterised by outbursts of verbal, physical, psychological or sexual abuse from the perpetrator towards their victim in an attempt to dominate them with domestic abuse. This may also be done by destroying their victim's property. On more than one occasion have I worked with a victim where this has happened and in most of these incidents, the victim's belongings have been destroyed whilst the perpetrator's own property is left in pristine condition.

The most common thing that a perpetrator will do during this stage is to express to their victim that they had it coming to them and go on to lay the full blame of the incident at their feet.

During these outbursts, the victim will most certainly experience a degree of fear and, certainly within the early outbursts, they may try to defend themselves against the abuse or shout for help. However, my experience from those I have worked with is that as time goes on, the more and more times they go through the cycle, it is more about doing what is necessary to survive or to allow the incident to run its course and stop. The victims that have been in this position a number of times also talk about the burden that they feel on those that are trying to support them, their family and specialist services to name just two as they continue to go through the cycle.

Children who live in the home where there are these kinds of incidents are affected also, even if as so many claim that they never see the incidents. They may never see the actual incident but they can and do hear it, and they do feel the "air of tension" that exists also. We will talk more about children later on, as some of the stories I have had shared with me are quite literally heart breaking.

Reconciliation:

During the reconciliation phase, the perpetrator will more often than not claim to feel sadness or remorse over what happened. I also believe truly that this is more to do with fear that they may be feeling about their victim reporting their behaviour to the police, at least in the early days. They will offer up an apology in some shape or form but also continue to place the blame over what happened on the victim by saying things like "I really am sorry about what I did but if you hadn't looked at that woman the way you did in the shop, this wouldn't have happened. How do you think that made me feel?"

I have also heard from survivors that I have worked with that their perpetrators have threatened to harm themselves or even to commit suicide if they left them in an attempt to get sympathy from them or to ensure that they stay in the relationship due to guilt they may well be feeling. I feel it is important, however, to point out to those who are experiencing this that perpetrators who threaten to take their own lives in this situation seldom do, but it is their main tactic to make you stay. Looking at suicide, those that do take their lives rarely talk of their plans or make threats to do so, they take action. The guilt that this tactic makes you feel isn't yours to bear, it's a controlling tactic aimed to keep you "in line". You are worth so much more than this existence.

In most cases, they will certainly make promises to their victim that this type of behaviour won't happen again and also play down the extent of what they did by trying to convince their victim that it wasn't as bad as they are making out the incident was. Perpetrators of abuse can be very convincing during this period and their victims who are so eager to rekindle those "good times" that they have experienced, or they have become so worn down by long-standing abuse, they accept that maybe they do have to shoulder some of the blame or that maybe they are making "a mountain out of a mole hill" and stay within the relationship. This blame is not yours to hold on to; you are your own person and deserve a life of freedom, respect and love.

Calm:

This phase has also been referred to as the "honeymoon period" and is generally characterised by the perpetrator trying to create a normal environment so that the incident can be put behind them and regain control within the relationship. They will generally go one of two ways; either acting as though nothing has happened in a hope that their victim will fall back in line (an example of gas lighting which we will explore later) or they will do things such as buy presents, become more intimate or take part in activities their victim likes to do. This leads the victim to believe that maybe this time they have changed but sadly this is not the case, as over a period of time, new issues will arise moving the cycle back into the tension-building phase.

One notable thing that came from the majority of the male victims I have known and worked with is that as the relationship progresses and passes time and time again through the cycle of abuse, the calm stage reduces in length (or time that it lasts) until it gets to the point that they go from reconciliation directly back to tension-building as they know it is only a matter of time before it starts again. Some may think that once the calm stage starts to reduce, surely victims would leave. The truth is that as this period gets shorter, the more it is desired and treasured by the victim as it is the times they enjoy. This leaves them living for these moments, as fleeting and scarcer they become over time.

Being Set Up:

Now it has been known for a perpetrator of abuse to set their victim up as a way of moving around the cycle of abuse.

This was not a concept that I was familiar with until a survivor I worked with told me about an incident he had with his partner once that lead to her threatening him with a weapon in their kitchen. He maintained that he did not know if she would ever have used the weapon but he was genuinely fearful for his life.

He had on more than one occasion been accused of having a bit of a thing for the young girl that worked in their local shop, purely on the back of one conversation with her over the car she had bought and he was told by his partner that she wasn't blind and could see that the girl quite clearly had a thing for him too. This had been going on for a while and on one occasion, after the same accusations he had been facing regularly, he was asked by his partner to go to the shop as they had run out of coffee. On his way to the shop, he had got stuck in some road works which had delayed him by no more than 10 minutes than it would usually take.

On returning home, as he walked through the door, he started trying to apologise for taking so long and to explain about the road works but as he turned, a shoe was thrown at him and he was greeted with a barrage of abuse from his partner. She accused him of being a liar and that she had known that something was going on with the girl from the shop and now she had all the proof she needed as it shouldn't take so long to get to the shop and back. He followed her into the kitchen trying to explain that this wasn't the case and that the girl hadn't even been at the shop but this had made the matter worse. His partner had turned back to him with a weapon in hand, again accusing him of being a lair and making a fool out of her in front of everyone, she went on to make several threats of violence towards him and herself if he didn't come clean and admit what he had been doing. So even though he had done absolutely nothing wrong, he apologised to her and agreed that what she had suspected was right and that he did have a thing for the girl at the shop in an attempt to bring the incident to a close. But even though after a lot of apologising on his behalf and agreeing that he wouldn't go to that shop again (even though he had done nothing in the first place), the incident moved on through the phases, and it was used as a go-to trigger point for further incidents in the future.

When reflecting on this incident with this survivor, he had initially thought it had been brought about by insecurities his partner had. But he came to the realisation that the accusations and then being asked to go to the shop was all part of a well-constructed plan that his partner had put together to instigate an "incident" within their relationship.

What is important to remember when within an abusive relationship is that the perpetrator will never change their behaviour unless something is done about it. The cycle will continue until their victim either leaves, seeks help or in the extreme cases the victim loses their life.

Chapter Three
Introducing the Perpetrator

So, what type of person does it take to be a perpetrator of abuse? What sort of background do they come from? What experiences have made them behave in the way they do today?

Perpetrators can come from a whole host of backgrounds; just like with their victims there isn't a blueprint for them. I have come across a variety of different people that have perpetrated abuse. A head teacher, a housewife/mother, a dog trainer, a model, the list is endless. The only thing that is for certain is that they have a desire to offend, to hurt, to humiliate and frustrate. More importantly, they desire to disempower and scare their chosen victim. They will always use manipulation and guilt; they will employ the use of blackmail, male stereotypes and threats of a variety of nature to control. Contrary to what most believe, female perpetrators of abuse will resort to violence, just as their male equivalent do, and are more likely to use a weapon when they do. Much that can be read on the internet speaks of how female perpetrators of abuse are only doing so as a reaction to the abuse that they are suffering within the relationship. It is recognised that violence resistance does happen (not just with female victims as I have worked with men who have ended up with custodial sentences for defending themselves from a physical attack) but to state that this is always the case is just untrue.

The female perpetrator will many times use manipulation to make their victim believe that they are the reason for the violence giving substance to what is written, that it was something their victim said, did or didn't do that is the reason behind this behaviour. But this could not be further from the truth. Everyone is responsible for their own actions, their own thoughts, their own feelings and nothing that someone else does justifies or is an excuse for abuse.

So just why do abusive people feel they need to have control over someone? Could it be that deep down, they could feel insecure or afraid of being alone? Could it be that they themselves feel isolated? Does this matter? Does it in any way justify their behaviours? There are many different theories offered up to explain the reasons behind domestic abuse, but not many that look at the experiences of male victims.

If we look at some of the things that male survivors have told me when I was working with them, there really are some outdated beliefs that female perpetrators live by. One of the most common that came up on a number of occasions was that it was the man's job to provide, I mean what sort of a man can't provide for his family, after all? I myself thought we had evolved, but maybe I was wrong. There is just something very archaic about that belief, is there not? It just sounds so very hunter/gather. As part of this belief, they also think that they shouldn't be expected to hold down a job as it is their role to raise the children and that their partner should do all he can to ensure their happiness (even though we've evolved and moved on from the nuclear family).

I racked my brain to think of and find examples of where this belief comes from and found my answer purely by accident over Christmas. The stereotypical family where the man goes to work and the woman stays home to cook, clean and raise the children is the basis behind one of my favourite films, *'It's a Wonderful Life'*, and there are so many films that also show this as the way things are in society. But if you look to when these films were made, it was back in era where this actually was how things were for the majority of families. Think about your grandparents, most of them when they were younger would have done this and maybe even your parents. I know that this is how things have been in my house up until the present when my wife returned to work, as we had two young children. The difference is that we discussed it and came to a joint decision; my wife didn't just assume that this would be the way it was.

Television and film do have a lot to answer for when it comes to gender stereotyping; as in most films we see these days, the central male character is portrayed as strong, and showing little emotion. When I was a kid, the two men that were seen as "real men" were Grant and Phil Mitchell on EastEnders. Well, if that's the definition of a real man then there was never any hope for me! But that's the thing, when we can't match up to what television and other media says we should be, as a victim of abuse it can be used against us. I have heard more times than I care to recount men that I have known being told to "man up" (which to me is a massively abusive thing to say as it basically is holding men to old outdated standards by saying we are not behaving like a man) or things like "if you can't give me what I want, I'll find a real man that can."

As I have already alluded to, these sorts of beliefs that this is the norm in society are very outdated now, times have changed. We've had the era of girl power and quite rightly more equality within a relationship. I myself have plenty of male friends who believe in equality and actually do the stay-at-home dad thing when their children are young as their partners are in better-paid jobs. And the real truth is that they wouldn't trade the experience of the early years with their kids. But that in itself was frowned upon not that long ago when it wasn't socially acceptable for the man to play "mum" whilst his partner worked and that also was a potential reason for abuse as stay-at-home dads were considered lazy, stupid and weak. How wrong could those people be to think this way? I once worked with a man in his early 20's who was being abused by is partner, who he had two young children with. Despite the abuse he suffered, he would not hear a word said against her or fault her as a mother in any way as she looked after the children whilst he worked and he believed she did a good job. Over the years, he had moved up the ladder significantly in his role into quite a senior position but it transpired that his partner wasn't caring for the children as well as he thought. One day when he returned home, he was greeted by a social worker who advised he was faced with the real possibility of his children being taken into care due to neglect. This was the turning point for him and what he had been going through as he felt he had let his children down. He disclosed the abuse to the social worker and made a statement to the police, who did everything they could to protect him and his children. Within days, he had handed in his notice at work and stepped out into the unknown world as a single dad. I would like to say he was supported well in taking on this role but fact was, he learnt by himself. He went to children's centres, parenting classes and asked as many fathers as he could for advice. This is a real man to me and a real inspiration to all.

Anyhow, I've moved off track which will probably happen a lot as I want to share as many experiences and stories with you as I can, for I believe it helps you to see that you truly are not alone.

Back to the perpetrator then, as well as their very misguided beliefs, she has a full arsenal of reasons to justify why she has done the things she has, especially during the reconciliation period after an incident. The three most common that I have come across would be:

- Alcohol ("I was drunk, I couldn't help it." or "If it wasn't for you, I wouldn't have to drink, so take some responsibility for what you've done.")
- Time of the month ("You try controlling your emotions when your hormones are all over the place!")
- Children ("It's alright for you, you go off to work whilst I'm stuck here. You try looking after them, they've been on at me all day!")

Again, I ask the question, does this justify the behaviour they are showing towards their victims? Does the fact that it's the "wrong time of the month" make up for the fact you've just had something thrown at you or been slapped? I'm hoping that I'm not alone here but I know more people that go through this period without raising a hand to their partner than I do those that become abusive. Most the women I know just become a little more emotional during this time, which is fine, it's a natural occurrence. I'm not going to talk any more about children or alcohol though, as there will be plenty explored around these areas of the book when we look at tactics of abuse later on.

Ultimately it boils down to this, there is no justifiable cause for anyone being abusive and those that say otherwise are just making excuses. Making excuses because they know that their behaviour is wrong and they wish to deflect away from this. The bottom line is that they do what they do for power and control over their victim.

Power and Control:

Any relationship that can be described as a good relationship will always be based on equality and respect between partners. But when one partner uses different tactics to gain control over the other, the results can be damaging as it causes a power imbalance. Power and control within an intimate relationship was clearly described by the Duluth Power and Control Wheel that was developed in 1981 by the Minnesota Domestic Abuse Intervention Project to explain the nature of abuse and tactics used. The problem was that it was created before there was an understanding or even the belief that men could be victims and focussed on a man's use of violence within an abusive relationship. Tom Graves later developed a modified, or inverted model if you like, designed as a gender-neutral description of perpetrators of abuse which is the one that I'm going to share with you. This in itself give a whole new insight into the dynamics of an abusive relationship:

- Using intimidation
- Using emotional abuse
- Using isolation
- Minimising, denying, blaming
- Using children
- Using gender privilege
- Using economic abuse
- Using coercion and threats

What I want to do is to take a little look at each of the sections just to give a bit of an insight into what they mean. I will be going in to a lot more depth once I start looking at the tactics of abuse in the upcoming chapters.

- Using coercion and threats is when a perpetrator forces their victim to do something they wouldn't usually do by making threats against them. This could be threats of violence, threats against other relatives or family members (including children) or even threats of false allegations. The perpetrator is attempting to gain compliance from their victim through the use of intimidation.
- Using intimidation is basically what it says on the tin. It's about intentional behaviours designed to make someone fearful of injury or harm. This doesn't have to be characterised by violence as certain looks or gestures can be intimidating.
- Using emotional abuse aims to reduce the victims' confidence and self-esteem in an attempt to make them more dependent on their perpetrator. Sadly,

most survivors of this type of abuse have said that the impact is worse than any physical abuse they have suffered and can take much longer to recover from.

- Using isolation cuts the victim off from the outside world which reduces the opportunity for the victim to disclose what is happening to them and to reduce their opportunities to flee from the abuse.

- Minimizing, denying, blaming is about the perpetrator playing down the levels of abuse that they have displayed and shifting the responsibility for the abuse to the victim.

- Using children is probably the tactic that is used that I struggle with the most. It is when the children are either used as a tool to abuse or as a weapon against the victim, an example would be stopping the victim from seeing them.

- Using gender privilege can be looked at in a number of ways such as acting like the mistress of the house and making the important decisions without consultation. She would also make a point that she could make accusations and services would side with her.

- Using economic abuse can be defined as interfering or controlling their victims' access to economic resources such as food, money or transport. It is used to create financial insecurities so as to limit the victims' financial means to flee to safety.

All of these we will look at in more detail through the various stages of abuse when I aim to go into more detail about the types of behaviours that female perpetrators show to their male victims. This will be invaluable to those who may be facing many of these behaviours but not realising that they are being abused. It will also be of value to family members and professionals, to better understand what male victims are facing on a daily basis. As I said in the foreword, I once took part in a course as a facilitator where we looked at the alternative to the Power and Control Wheel but with examples of the behaviours included on it. What struck me the most was when my co-facilitator asked the men in the room to tick off what they had experienced, and one by one they started ticking away all the different examples of abuse on their worksheets.

So, without delaying any further, let's take a look at the tactics employed by a female perpetrator. These are the areas we are going to explore and the behaviours you may be or have been experiencing:

- Emotional and psychological abuse
- Physical abuse
- Economic abuse
- Sexual abuse
- Using isolation
- Using children
- Drugs and alcohol

Chapter Four
Emotional and Psychological Abuse

When we think about domestic abuse, the first thought or vision that usually pops into our heads will be that of physical violence from a man to a woman. That is probably due to the fact that up until recent years, it was still referred to as domestic violence and some still call it that now. When it comes to male perpetrators, I agree that more likely than not, you are looking at many of them using physical forms of abuse and it being one of the most common, if not the most common. Women, however, tend to favour a different approach when they perpetrate abuse, mainly in the form of emotional and psychological abuse which makes the abuse much harder to detect (this again raises that question of 1 in 6 males being victims if it is truly harder to detect). A member of my survivor group once said that they would rather be physically assaulted by their partner as those scars are likely to heal but the emotional abuse suffered over the years and its psychological effects could last a lifetime. It's a sad thought that someone could feel this way, isn't it, which has stuck with me ever since.

One of the most common ways that this type of abuse is perpetrated towards males is by name calling and putting them down, on the surface that may not sound bad, some of you may even be thinking "really?" but when done continuously over a period of time, it does have negative effects on the victim. It could be things like telling them that they are too fat, making comments like "don't you think you should lose a few pounds? It's starting to get embarrassing being seen with you." I hear that one a lot with the male victims I talk to, I myself had this, and in some cases this negative image they were having placed on them has led onto quite serious eating disorders. Hard to believe for some I know, but men do have emotions too and comments about our weight can affect us in exactly the same way as it does for some women. The body shaming comments are just one of the many personal traits of their victim that female perpetrators will use to try and make their victim feel ugly in some way. Quite literally, anything that she can use about our physical appearance will be used. Here are just a few others that I have encountered. Take someone with a beard, it could be comments about them looking like a vagrant, or someone who is shorter than their partner could be subjected to plenty of comments about coming up short to the mark when it comes to being a man. You name it, I've probably heard it from one of the numerous men I have worked with as something that has been aimed towards them. This is just one example of the types of things that come up in an attempt to put someone down, when the perpetrator is guilty of trying to strip their victim of their self-esteem. There is the other side of it when men are just outright called abusive names like prick, twat and wanker, just to pick off a few from the many possibilities. Though this generally tends to be done in the privacy of the home and not when they are out in public or with friends. Why, you ask? Well, quite simply, the perpetrator has a separate persona to keep up in front of others. Just imagine for a minute, if you constantly have someone calling you names, it's going to have a massively detrimental effect on you, isn't it? If you are a victim of abuse reading this, you probably know what I'm talking about, as I would guess that you may have experienced this yourself.

One of the tactics that men tend to struggle with and find quite hurtful is when their partners attempt to make them feel like less of a man by making negative comments or statements about their penis size or their sexual performance. Comments about their penis being too small, like "what the hell is that? Do you think you could possibly give me any pleasure with that" or how much of a waste of time sex had been as their partner, who in their opinion was completely useless, even if they had actually enjoyed it, maybe saying things like "I could have had more fun on my own!" or "You owe me one." A client once said that this phrase alone has stuck with him and still affects him now. It has also been known for men to be verbally attacked by their partners for not being able to sexually perform. They would start arguments with them accusing them of being homosexual, as they clearly don't find them attractive otherwise this would not be a problem. One man I worked closely with was actually humiliated in front of all their friends by making what they claimed was a joke of this. What is important to remember is that stress and fear has a massive effect on a number of functions of the body, sexual desire and performance included. A victim of domestic abuse is under stress 24 hours a day, 7 days a week, so it would hardly be surprising for this to happen from time to time. When this is an issue, female perpetrators will more often than not be unfaithful to their victims and either tell their victim or when found out, will use this as an excuse. Sadly, quite often this act of being unfaithful will be with someone the victims know, maybe a friend or family member, which will also feed into isolation (which I will talk a lot more about in later chapters). One male survivor that I worked with once disclosed to us within a group session that it was commonplace that his partner would have other men around to the house and then lock him out when he would go out the back for a cigarette. He said that he didn't know if anything was happening between them but it was impossible to stop the kind thoughts that were going through his head, these were enough to drive anyone mad but to him, he believed there was nothing he could do and he just had to accept it. As a sort of buffer for this behaviour from them, it would not be massively uncommon for a female perpetrator to turn the tables on their partner and accuse their victim of being unfaithful, using the good old phrase "you're a man, it's what you all do!" and "you can't keep your dick in your pants!" This in itself can be extremely wearing on the emotional wellbeing of anyone being accused of having an affair, especially if you know that despite what you say, you will not be believed; especially in the context of an abusive relationship it can have massive detrimental effects on the victim emotionally.

As if all this we have covered already isn't enough for a male victim to cope with, the perpetrator will also compare them to other men, not just celebrities but others in their own neighbourhood environment too. When it comes to be compared with celebrities, this of course can happen to the victim night after night in most cases, as most people do sit and watch television for some part of every evening. It doesn't matter what the programme, it could be singers, footballers, boxers, actors, they will find someone to compare their victim with. Little passing comments that will be made by the perpetrator like "why don't you look more like him? I bet he knows how to please a woman and keep her happy". On a night-by-night basis, this is wearing and any enjoyment that was once gained by watching television will be lost. As I just said though, it's not just celebrities; it could equally be someone within her own environment, a new neighbour moving in for example, "he's a bit of alright, if only you could carry yourself like him". This could lead to the victim witnessing their partner talking to and maybe even spending more time with this neighbour as a way to torture them.

As another tactic of emotional abuse, humiliation can also play a key role and what is interesting is just how clever female perpetrators of abuse are at this. I've already shared an example of this and one thing that is certain, she will have no problem using your fears against you to humiliate in front of people. Take the spider, your normal every-day household spider. How many people do you know within your lives who have a phobia of spiders? It's one of the most common phobias in the world for someone to have; I myself am not by any means their biggest fan. But the perpetrator will use this phobia and make light of this to get others laughing at their victim. Take a situation where they might be around others and someone will notice that there is a spider in the room, she will deliberately make a point of telling everyone not to ask their victim to get rid of it as he is "a bit of a big girl's blouse and likely to run away screaming like a girl". Plenty of men I know that have experienced this have said after a few times they gave up defending themselves when this happened as their partner would tell them that they needed to get a grip as they were only joking, always in front of everyone, causing their victim to feel guilt and a deeper sense of humiliation than they did at the outset. They will also make jokes about things their victims have done around the house, again causing people to laugh at them. I once worked with a chef, a really nice bloke who was very good at what he did, I should know I have eaten at the place he works many times but his partner would always tell friends that they had invited for dinner that she had cooked, as despite the fact he was apparently a professional chef, all he could be bothered to cook at home was a microwave dinner. Apparently, once and only once, one of her friends had questioned this and said that she should cut him a bit of slack as she could understand him not wanting to cook; who would when they had been doing it all day? Well, this friend never got an invite to dinner again.

Many will agree with me when I say DIY is a great British pastime for men, but it also seems to be another popular choice when it comes to criticism for male victims. Anyone who has ever visited my home bears witness to the fact that I am shocking at most DIY and will tell you that there isn't one shelf that is 100% straight, which is fine, they still do their job. But for your male victim, in the same situation with wonky shelves, a perpetrator will refuse to use them and point out how bad they are to anyone who will listen, sometimes commenting on how much of a waste of space their partner is as they never get anything right. All of this is done within earshot of their victim who had taken the time and effort to try to put them up.

Another tactic of emotional and psychological abuse is that of gas lighting, which is an American term and is potentially the most harmful for victims. I can hear what you are thinking, one simple word "what?" This is common in victims as in many other people that are unaware of what this tactic of abuse is. Gas lighting is when a perpetrator is gaining more power and control over their victim by distorting their sense of reality in the relationship. Over the course of an abusive relationship, the more this happens, it wears you down until you are more likely than not to accept the abuser's distorted perception of the truth. To put things simply, they are trying to make their victims believe that they are losing the plot, that they are going mad. The term gaslight originates from the 1940s film of the same title where the husband attempts to convince his wife that she is insane by manipulating things within the home. In modern domestic abuse relationships, gas lighting generally is done by hiding things, making the victim think they have forgotten things and the blame game (which is basically saying it's your fault not mine).

Hearing stories about hiding things was always quite a frequent occurrence when I worked in the domestic abuse field. I remember clearly the story one male told me about his car keys going missing at home and what he discovered. See this man, by his own admission, would lose his keys (as well as his phone and other things but we are talking about his keys), not that he had really lost them as they were always in his coat or bag. Because of this, he decided that to reduce the chance of this happening again he would put a bowl on the shelf inside the door to keep them in. This he did religiously every day and it became part of his routine. On one occasion, as he was about to go out in the evening, he went to the bowl and his keys weren't there which confused him as he thought he remembered putting them in, so he asked his partner if she had seen them, which she denied she had. He then went on a search of the house, retracing every step since he got home and but still could not find them. Just as he was about to give up any hope of finding them, he passed the bowl again and there they were. He knew in his mind that they weren't there a minute ago so again he asked his partner if she had put them there, she got very defensive asking what he was accusing her of and that they clearly must have been there before, that he just hadn't looked properly. This was the first of many times this happened and this man genuinely believed he was starting to lose the plot until one day whilst searching for his keys, he happened to come around the corner of the stairs at the exact moment his partner was putting his keys back in the bowl. He waited for her to return to where she had been sitting, getting what he had seen clear in his mind before he asked her if she had put them back in the bowl which she denied, even though he had seen her do it. When he told her that he had seen her putting them back, she again became very defensive and said that they had been left on the coffee table and she had done it on this occasion as she hadn't wanted him to feel bad about his failing memory. So, she claimed it was a one-off and in terms of proof of all the other times, he had none. But after this day his keys never went missing again, his bank card and other items did but never his keys. Coincidence?

By making the victim think that they have forgotten important things also slowly but surely grind them down. Certainly, within the early stages of an abusive relationship it is not uncommon for the perpetrator to play down the extent of an incident by making comments like "I never said/did that" or "what are you on about? That never happened." She may try to convince her victim that she had told them information about important dates which their victim had quite clearly has forgotten. This tactic will quite often lead on to being asked "don't you care? It doesn't seem like you do" which also leads into blame being used as a tactic as it moves the focus directly off them and securely onto the victim.

Blame is the perpetrators' most favourite weapon when it comes to them perpetrating gas lighting as a tactic, they are projecting the blame of their actions onto the victim is their escape route from being held accountable for their actions. They may put the blame on their victim by saying that they saw the way they had looked at another woman, that they are always flirting and they thought she didn't know, similar to the set-up story we looked at earlier.

It is exhausting living with and dealing with a gas lighter as they will leave their victim feeling that they quite literally are losing their mind. One thing is certain about the victim, they'll be losing sleep which itself will impact their energy and will undoubtedly see a decrease in their mental health, possibly to the point of depression. For men, facing emotional domestic abuse could lead to one of the many cases of suicide we see in males in this country; for others, it could see a visit to their doctors to discuss their concerns about their mental health. This is another situation where a perpetrator can use a situation to their advantage by actively encouraging the victim to go to and then using these professionals against them, in this case a doctor, to further the belief that they are either losing the plot or just seriously depressed. Living with this type of behaviour that we have been looking at will undoubtedly make the victim feel depressed anyway, I think it would with anyone, but if the doctor agrees that they are suffering with depression, the perpetrator will then use that against them. I've been told by one survivor about how this is exactly what happened to him. His partner became very controlling when his mental health started to take a dip, not letting him go anywhere. She insisted that they attend a doctor's appointment together to discuss about his recent memory problems and their joint concerns about his mental health. He agreed to this but after he had finished his consultation with the doctor, his wife asked him to leave the room and sit in the waiting area whilst she speaks to the doctor alone. They were talking alone for some time and to this day, despite a number of requests for this to be disclosed, he has no idea what was said between his wife and the doctor, but the result was that he was put onto a course of anti-depressants and a note attached to his medical records about the issues with his mental health. This has come back to haunt him on several occasions since that time where this information was used against him, certainly when it came to child contact.

Female perpetrators of emotional and psychological abuse will also use what I have come to refer as the gender card when it comes to their tactics. One of the most common things I have heard that female perpetrators have said to male victims is that no one will believe them if they report what has been happening as it only happens to women. They will point to things like size difference between them, their victims' mental health, and any number of things as to why they wouldn't be believed. Also, the other thing is telling them that there is no one to help them should they leave, that they have nowhere to go anyway, that they would have no money to survive and ultimately because of this, they need them, as services don't help men. My belief is that this alone is a great example of how referring to domestic abuse as a "gendered crime" could be detrimental to male victims, and actually stop them from coming forwards. I mean, why would they? This message is just reiterating what their perpetrator has been telling them for some time.

There are three feelings that a perpetrator using emotional abuse is trying to trigger within a male victim; these are anxiety, fear and guilt. Anxiety is defined as the experience of fear without the object of the fear being there. The anxiety itself is caused by a lot of projection as to what could happen, somebody winding the victim up or in fact the victim winding themselves up with thoughts of what is to come. Perpetrators of abuse use this anxiety to control their victims by gently tugging on any insecurity they have or by making references to something negative that may or may not happen in the future.

Fear is used to control the victim by the perpetrator doing what they can to raise the victim's fear levels, think about the cycle of abuse at tension-building stage, the fear that the victim experiences must be quite an intense feeling. I mean just think of all the things they must be fearful of; fear of disapproval or making a mistake due to previous experience of the known consequences, fear of the conflict, the anger and the resulting confrontation. Once the victim has become fully isolated by their perpetrator, they will also be feeling a fear of rejection, abandonment and the resulting isolation, by this stage the only person they have left to depend on in their lives is their perpetrator.

It may be a struggle to see how guilt can fit into these feelings but understanding how female perpetrators behave and what guilt is, helps to explain this. Guilt is something that a person feels as a result of feeling responsible for the emotions and experiences of others. Guilt is effectively utilised by the female perpetrator very well, those facial expressions she uses, the look of hurt when the victim doesn't do what she has asked and the sulking that follows, yet stating "nothing is wrong". She will also be guilty of reversing the roles and playing the victim, making out she does everything for the victim yet they can't do one simple thing for them in return and finally the ultimate way to use guilt is through crying. Look at all of these potential ways that a female perpetrator can and does use guilt against a male. Can anybody say that if any of these were used against them, they wouldn't feel guilty? I know I would. Female perpetrators are extremely good at using the threat of self-harm and suicide, as they know this does impact massively on the male victim as despite what they have been subjecting them to, they do care for them and they certainly don't want their partner to harm themselves.

But it isn't just these threats about themselves they can make that plays on the emotional side of their victim, they also make threats to harm or kill their partner and when this doesn't have the desired effect, they will also make threats about their close family or to their pets. I have heard stories of perpetrators telling their victims that one of their close family members has died when they hadn't just to cause them emotional distress and hurt. I also worked with a man whose partner had a suspicion that he was going to leave and text him to say that if he did, the next time he would see his dogs would be their severed heads delivered in a box. Female perpetrators can and have threatened some pretty vile things in an attempt to keep their victim under their control. They will also make threats towards friends that the victim may have, like accusing the friend of rape which can lead to the victim trying to do whatever they can from keeping them from coming around, even though when they do, the perpetrator will act like they really like them. To my knowledge, these types of threat have never been followed through, but that's not saying it hasn't happened. But threats of this kind towards the victim can happen and have been followed up on.

There was a male I worked with who was planning to flee from his relationship. I remember one of the first things he ever said was about the threats that she had made towards him, which was that if he ever tried to leave her, she would go to the police, accuse him of rape and make sure she ruined his life. I kept a record of this as I believed this to be important and also advised him that if such an accusation was made, they would have to investigate as it is an accusation of a serious crime. On the day that he fled the home address to a new address that we had helped him to secure, she did exactly what she had threatened when she realised that he had gone and he was arrested. He spent just over 24 hours in custody whilst they investigated and eventually all charges were dropped against him as she just upped and left the area. Certainly, for an accusation like this, things could have been so much worse for him than they ended up being, but again this trauma that he was put through really affected him.

One final threat that a female perpetrator can make that can have a serious effect on their victim, is to leave them. This you may think would be a welcome threat, but for those that have been subjected to the abuse for some time and have become dependent on their partner, the threat of this can be crippling for them. Furthermore, add a child to the mix, a threat to leave comes hand in hand with taking the children which is possibly the worst threat that could be made against them.

So, for a man who is experiencing emotional abuse on a regular, if not daily, basis, what impact does it actually have on them? Well, for starters they will certainly have developed a degree of doubt in themselves which in turn will affect their self-esteem; I don't think anyone that experiences this type of abuse could not be affected in this way. Men who have suffered emotional abuse over a number of years may really struggle to show their emotions as this would be used against them and they may turn to substances as a way to cope with how they are feeling. Also because of this treatment they have suffered from their partners it will make them very untrusting of other people which does affect ongoing relationships in the future once they have left that relationship.

I have also touched on the subject of suicide earlier in this chapter; however, this should not be understated. It is known that if we look at the statistics around suicide, men are the most likely victims. But just how many of these cases are as a result of domestic abuse? Who can surely know unless there is some sort of note left behind? But one thing can't be ignored, and that is that in the England and Wales last year, 4,303 men took their own lives. Think about all the behaviours we looked at in this chapter alone, without even taking into account all the other types of abuse, and is suicide not possibly a real thought for many on these victims as a means of escape? Even if only 1% of this statistic were victims of domestic abuse, that would be 43 men per year, but my personal belief is that the percentage is probably much higher.

But moving forward, all is not lost as there are things that male survivors can do to address some of the feelings they have been living with which I would like to share with you:

- Learning to accept your feelings and not try to block it out. We all have feelings and that is OK, we need to accept that.
- Learning that we all have our limitations, unless of course you are Superman (but even he had limitations to kryptonite).
- Take small steps as nobody can go from feeling zero to a hundred over-night. You need to be able to have time to define your own morals and understand what you stand for.
- Become assertive as this helps you to deal with emotions. Being assertive helps you to express yourself and stand up for your beliefs, but at the same time respecting those of others.
- Find things that you can do that hep you deal with those feelings like anxiety and fear. It could be cycling; it could be fishing which is quite popular with the men I worked with. It could be that you need to ask yourself if there was anything you used to do that stopped because of the abusive relationship and rekindle that lost passion you had for an activity.
- Try to change your own reactions to negative feelings, accept the feeling but don't just sit with it. Don't let the negative feeling control your life.

Access to services such as counselling can help you to learn how to express yourself.

Remember we all need a chance to feel relaxed but you cannot feel relaxed whilst dealing with the negative emotions experienced at the hands of an emotional abuser. For those that feel that there is no way out, there are always options and people that you can reach out to for help.

Chapter Five
Men Bleed Too (Physical Abuse)

Although not perceived to be as prevalent with male victims of abuse as it is with female victims, physical abuse still does play a significant part when it comes to the abuse on men. As with the other types of abuse, when you mention physical violence in a relationship, most people will picture a woman being hit by their male partner but not the other way around. Organisations and individuals have run a number of different social experiments across the country as well, some of which you can see on YouTube, where this was explored and, in most cases, the results were the same. When the video showed a man was grabbing his partner and raising his voice, members of the public stopped and intervened, but when the roles were reversed, everyone either blanked on what was happening or sat, watched and laughed. I ask one question, how is either different? How is one acceptable and not the other?

It is almost impossible not to view acts of physical aggression as exactly what they are, but there are other aspects to physical abuse that you may not have even considered and these may well be happening to you. If this is the case, as you go through this chapter, it is quite possible that some or all of what we will discuss has or is happening to you.

If we start by looking at physical abuse in terms of physical contact, it is a fact that men can and do get punched by their female partners. Many believe that factors such as size difference and that a man generally is built to be significantly stronger will prevents this from happening, but this is a falsehood. One of the men I used to work with told me a story from when he was on holiday with his now ex-partner. He explained that the first part of the week had been fine so he started letting his defences down a bit as he felt he could relax for the first time in a very long time. His partner had suggested to him that they enter a couple's competition where they could win a free holiday which he was completely in agreement with. He said that he thought they had both enjoyed it, even though they lost by one question, but the minute they got back to their accommodation, he turned from closing the door to be greeted by a punch to the side of his face. This knocked him to the floor and she repeatedly punched him in the top of his head numerous times accompanied by a torrent of abuse, this because she blamed him for costing her a free holiday.

The thing is, men in general are three times less likely to disclose abuse than women, and if physically assaulted, it is a lot less likely due to the feeling of shame and humiliation. The results of this are the stories of "walking into doors" or "tripping over something", which are becoming much more common from male victims.

Some of the more common ways known that women physically abuse men are by slapping them. Certainly, there is less chance of bruising being caused than a punch but it does cause quite a bit of pain, I know, I myself have experienced this. They will also physically push them around and pull their hair, usually whilst subjecting them to a torrent of verbal abuse. For most men that I have worked with that have reported this, it was in response to something that they apparently didn't do and was accompanied by name calling like "useless" or them saying things like "do you just not listen or are you just fucking stupid?" Slightly more extreme than this, that I have come across and seen the resulting marks left behind, is the victim being bit, scratched and pinched. This does leave a lasting mark for a period of time on the victim and is usually done in a place that cannot be seen such as the underside of the arm or the sides. Let's also not forget her kicking her victim as a way to physically punish them. This can be slight kicks to the legs or sides, just letting them know that she is not happy or kicking in a violent and aggressive way, maybe to the head or to the genitals. This does happen, I have listened to more than one male explain how when they were asleep, their partner had violently kicked them there to wake them up, as a way of punishing them for something that happened in the day or, as one man's experience, for apparently calling out another woman's name in his sleep.

That covers the majority of what I can only describe as body-to-body physical abuse, but it doesn't stop there as I'm sure you are aware. The use of weapons, certainly when there is a male victim, does happen quite frequently. It can be smaller objects that get thrown at him such as ashtrays (less frequent now than it used to be) or it can be serious offensive weapons such as knives or screwdrivers. Any of these objects have the potential to cause serious harm to anyone, but in the hands of a perpetrator, this can lead to worse and the victim can lose their life. One of the most common weapons, which is really worrying, is the use of hot substances like boiling water, which seems to be increasingly a weapon of choice for female perpetrators. Many times, I have heard of hot drinks being dropped or poured over them for no other reason than to make them suffer. I would like to share a few of the experiences some of the men that I have worked with have been through themselves.

One that I remember clearly was a perpetrator whose choice of weapon was a lit cigarette. She would on a number of occasions burn his arms or legs when he wasn't looking and laugh about it. For him, the worst incident was when she flicked a lit cigarette end in his face that actually hit him in the eye. He was in pain for two days before he went to the doctor to get it looked at. It had burnt his eyelid which he was give some ointment for and when the doctor questioned him about it, he said he forgot he had a cigarette in his hand when he rubbed his face. Why had he said this? He explained that because his partner was sat opposite him, glaring at him, and the fear of repercussions he had left no choice but to lie.

Another experience that was shared with me was from a gentleman whose partner was arrested for assault and at the time was waiting to be taken to court. They had been out for a night and after a lot of alcohol, started to argue. As he was embarrassed by this, he suggested they leave and went home. On reflection, he wishes that he hadn't as whilst out, there were others around, but away from where they had been, there were times with nobody around. As the arguments intensified, it was at one of these times with nobody around that she removed her stiletto shoe and hit him in the chest with it. He was attended by an ambulance that was called by someone that had found him and rushed into surgery with the shoe heal stuck in his chest.

These are just two incidents out of a great number that have been shared with me and, although physical abuse isn't quite as common as emotional abuse, it does still happen and when it does happen, the results are a lot more severe, especially in these types of cases. I have heard stories where female perpetrators have used quite extreme weapons such as hitting their victims around the head with small televisions sets, smashing the screen in the process and even throwing small household appliances at them, in one case a small counter top freezer was thrown.

Something else that I have come across that also is considered physical abuse, although many do not think of, is that of withholding food and medication. With food, this is a basic need that we have to meet in order to survive. Without it, our bodies become weak and will ultimately shut down. This has been used as a tactic of physical abuse on a great number of occasions as when done, the male victim becomes weaker and weaker over a period of time, therefore, more likely to become compliant to the perpetrator's demands. I have heard stories of men being denied food for a few days as they "didn't deserve any" and being made to sit at the table and watch as the perpetrator and sometimes their children ate. Just remembering these stories now fills me with emotion, just as it did when I first heard them, imagining how these males that this happened to felt. The victims with children would just smile, so as not to cause upset to them as they looked on. The withholding of medication is just as serious, as this is usually something that they need for a serious medical condition and without it comes the knowledge that they could actually die. Again, this can and is used by female perpetrators as a way to control their male victims, with this knowledge, they will do whatever it takes to be given their medication back.

The consequences of these behaviours can lead to a very serious outcome and the victim can become so weak or hurt so badly that they can, and in some cases do, die as a result of the physical abuse. In the UK, between March 2015 and March 2017, there were 65 male victims of domestic homicide and in 42 of those cases, their female partner or ex-partner was a suspect. Granted, the numbers that do die as a result of domestic abuse may not be as high as the numbers of female victims but any death is one death too many, regardless of their gender. Raising awareness of physical abuse and its potential consequences is just one way to try and bring these numbers down.

It doesn't begin and end with the actual physical assault on the victim though; in the build up to the incident there are a number of warning signs that the victim will recognise that anyone else would be oblivious to. Some may say these are predominantly tactics of emotional and psychological abuse, but the fact these incidents are part and parcel of the physical abuse they certainly warrant a mention here in this tactic.

The female perpetrator will undoubtedly stare or glare at him in an attempt to make him feel really uncomfortable and in most cases succeeding at this, just as I alluded to in one of the stories a moment ago. This is done out of sight of other people, maybe behind their backs when out of the home but when at home she could quite happily sit doing this for quite some time. To accompany this, her breathing might be different from normal, with her breathing heavily to make sure she has got his attention or a lot of huffing as my mother used to call it.

Within the home, it is possible that they may have a certain place that they go to or sit and then they behave in a particular way or make gestures towards the victim, that to the victim is a warning that something is going to happen and makes them anxiously think of what they have done. These gestures I talk about would be unnoticeable to other people but combined with the way they look at their victim, they will definitely recognise the warning. The perpetrator's body language will also change from being quite open to closed and guarded; if you were there, you may see them sat with their arms folded, tapping their foot or fingers whilst looking or glaring at their victim. As things progress and the incident gets closer, she may come close to their face whilst screaming or shouting at them, but equally as possible, her tone could be cold and flat, either way this puts the victim on edge as he will know what the likely outcome is from past experience, but as always have no idea at all when it will happen. This is no way to live for anyone. The final thing that you may see happen in this period is that she will either threaten to or actually harm any pets that the victim may have; for her, this is a way she can hurt him directly without laying a finger on him. Unfortunately, it's more common than I wish it was.

Following any incident, as with emotional and psychological abuse, the perpetrator will minimise what they have done by denying things weren't as bad as their victim is making out, that they are exaggerating, even if they haven't said anything. If they have sustained any injuries in the assault, they will also turn the blame for those on the victim, often claiming that they had hardly touched them and that it was their clumsiness that had caused them to fall and that it was that which caused the injury.

I recently watched a documentary around a real-life victim of domestic abuse who suffered from physical abuse and it really moved me. The policeman that had responded to the latest in a long line of incidents said that he knew something wasn't right by the injuries that the man had but when he talked to him, he maintained that he had done it to himself. It was only because the officer was persistent and wanted to talk with him alone that when he was taken out of the home, the victim disclosed the truth about what had happened. His partner was arrested on suspicion of assault that occasions actual bodily harm (or ABH) and he was taken to hospital for his injuries to be examined. At the hospital he was taken to, the doctors said that on examining him, he was no more than 10 days away from death. The police also bought him a burger meal on the way to a hotel they booked him into on discharge from hospital, which he sadly described as the best meal he had ever eaten as he couldn't remember the last time he had a proper cooked meal. I cried watching this as it just reminded me of so many of the men I have supported and made me think of all those that are unknown about, suffering the same treatment as he had.

So how does living with physical abuse and the tactics their perpetrator uses affect the victim? One thing I hope is apparent straight away and that is that they would never be able to relax properly as they never knew when the next incident was going to happen; therefore, it is like they are constantly in a state of walking on eggshells. I have actually come across cases where the victim has become abusive to others, this as a way of trying to keep some form of control in their life as they dare not disagree with anything their perpetrator may say. I have seen male victims become abusive to their parents and actually make threats towards their fathers for nothing at all. Over time, the male victim becomes completely controlled by their partner, and can start to believe that it has to be something they have done that makes her so aggressive, as a result they become apologetic for everything and spend a lot of their time apologising.

But we are all responsible for our own actions and make our own decisions to take those actions. Nothing that you have done warrants any kind of physical assault. So, if anything that you have read here has rung any bells in your own relationship, you are not alone. There are support agencies and individuals out there that can and will support you.

Chapter Six
Financial and Economic Abuse

In the definition of what constitutes domestic abuse, one of the five main categories of abuse is defined as financial abuse. Financial abuse involves the perpetrator using, or in most cases misusing, their victim's money which can limit their ability to be able to do the things they wish to do. Two of the most common examples of this that I have come across while working with male victims have been putting contracts into their partner's name (mobile phones is very common, but sometimes it gets worse) and using of their credit cards without gaining their permission. These I will come back to shortly but when in these sorts of situations, it can leave the victim with no money for the things that they need once they have paid what needs paying or compromises are being made and debts recurring over things like pay day loans or credit cards not being paid.

Economic abuse encompasses all that financial abuse is and then some, as it recognises that this goes further. For this chapter, I will start by looking deeper at what has already been raised as financial abuse and then go more into the other factors that make it economic abuse.

So where to start? It can look different based on different circumstances; if a victim is working or unemployed, it can make a difference in the tactics that she will use. But either way, the female perpetrator of abuse will probably insist on having a joint account under the guise of the money being paid directly into one place and then the household bills can be paid from there, but in truth, what she is actually doing is engineering a situation where she will take control over the household finances or make it easier to transfer funds to her own separate account.

Let's start by taking a look at some of the tactics of abuse faced by a working man. She will certainly hold the belief and insist that as he is working, it is his responsibility to "take care" of the households needs, I mean, everyone knows "that it's a man's job to provide for his family" and will do whatever she can to deny him access to money that he earns, not necessarily by saying no directly but by assuring that all his income is tied up in payments for household bills and other "essentials". As she is in control of the finances, she sees it as her job to make decisions when it comes to the finances and will make most of the major financial decisions alone, without the input of her partner. This could be decisions around and affecting the mortgage, household utility bills (signing up for the top packages with things like sky television) and as she has her partner's income as a joint income, she is able to take out things like store cards, credit cards and small loans. It is very easy for this stream of money to run up some pretty hefty debts in quite a short period of time, believe me; I've seen it in a number of cases.

One male shared his experience of this with me, which focuses around this issue. His partner when they met was someone who liked to spend money. He knew this from the outset; however, once they had moved in together, when he progressed within his job and his salary increased, so did her spending and store cards. She herself had her own job but, as described above, she had insisted on a joint account to cover the household bills, leaving them both with some money available for themselves. He said that the transition period of them moving in together was great, they got on really well to begin with; there was the odd little disagreement here and there but nothing that he worried too much about. He had no knowledge of her debts as the store cards she had were in her name and when she had amassed so much debt that she was struggling to pay it each month, she spoke to him about it for the first time and he agreed that they could refinance her debt into a joint loan by just paying more into the joint account to clear this each month. This was done and despite the fact it restricted some of the things he could do because of this new expenditure, their lives continued in a way that he believed better than before. But no more than six months later, he found himself in the same situation, having the same conversation. When he questioned what she had been doing, she laid the blame at his feet and indicated as he was working such long hours, she had to find ways to keep herself entertained. She also indicated that if he paid her as much attention as his job, this wouldn't have happened. The guilt that she made him feel made the decision for him to agree to refinance once again and to start working from home a little more. It was at this time that he realised that his partner's drinking had increased from what it used to be and she was drinking most evenings at least a bottle of wine. When he started to question this, the emotional abuse started to creep in a lot more, the name calling, making out he was useless at home, that all he was good for was paying what he was responsible for. Their physical relationship had at this point ceased, she had made him move into the spare bedroom of their house and refused him access to the television or anything else (even though he partly paid for it). He reported to us that on more than one occasion she had physically assaulted him for no reason and thrown things at him during a barrage of abuse when she was drunk. It was when he spoke to a colleague that he had been friends with for years about what was going on at home that they said her behaviour was nothing but abusive, that was the first time he stopped and recognised it for what it was. The friend offered him somewhere to go to and he made the decision that he needed to split from his partner. Sounds like the end of this story, doesn't it? Nowhere near unfortunately. When he told his partner he was leaving, she broke down, saying she had a problem with alcohol, that this was causing the situation and that she would commit suicide if he left her as she would have no one. He sat and spoke to her and she told him that her alcohol had become an issue, running up some substantial big debts that she was struggling to cope with. She promised that she would get help from the local service and that they could sort it out together. This he agreed to as he did genuinely still love her despite her behaviour and looking at their financial situation, said they could refinance one last time. So, the appointment was booked the following week, he arrived at the bank and was in with the bank manager but his partner wasn't there. When he called her, she said she had gotten stuck at work but would be there in about 20 minutes. It was at this point that the bank manager said that his credit was good enough to take the loan in his name alone. I think you can see where this is going already. Feeling on the spot, he agreed and then let his partner know what he had done. They met back at home and made a lot of calls to people and cleared off all the debts that night. Thanking him for what he had done, she also invited him to move back into their bedroom which he at the time saw as an improvement in their faltering relationship. Less than a week later, she told him that she didn't feel that this relationship was working and that she had been in a relationship with someone else for a while now and left. Left free of debt and leaving him owing over £18,000 that she refused to pay. There was nothing he could do; he willingly took out the loan and paid her debts for her.

Sadly, this sort of case is too common place, it seems that so many men that experience financial abuse end up in the same position of owing large debts that are in their names that they themselves didn't take out or run up in the first place but are now ultimately responsible for. Let's move on to look at some of the other things that can and do happen in this type of situation within an abusive relationship.

One of the issues that male victims that are employed seem to experience is that their partner will not let him know about any other family income that they may be claiming, this has been the case in a couple of situations that I have been involved in where the partner was the home maker and stayed at home to raise the children. What we are talking about here are things like universal credit claims and child benefit, things that can be claimed as additional income. When this is discovered and they asked about this money, it is a common response by their partner to say that this was money for her and the children and therefore no business of his, even though he bought the food for the household and everything that the children needed. In one case I am aware of, the victim later discovered that there was a massive overpayment of the benefits that he then had to subsidise. To top off this situation, he discovered that his partner had been gambling the majority of the money on online bingo sites and sites of a similar nature.

For those that aren't employed, things can be a lot worse. This could be either because their perpetrator is working and therefore provides the predominant amount of the income, therefore taking what he gets as a contribution to the household costs or it would be a joint benefit claim which she would be in control of the money that they got as it is limited. In this situation, anything he may want or need, he would have to seek her permission for and justify why she should allow him the money for it (and usually he wouldn't get it anyway). When this happens, he is left with absolutely no financial means of doing anything without depending on her for it all. Something that also can happen in this situation is that she can give him a set amount of money to do the week's shopping and then verbally abuse him when he doesn't get it all, knowing full well she hasn't given him enough in the first place.

So that's a bit of an overview on just some of the financial aspects. Now let's take a look at the parts of it that makes it economic abuse. Economic abuse isn't just about restricting money and running up debts; it's about restricting access to transport and the means to improve your economic status. In other words, preventing you from further education, training or getting and keeping meaningful employment.

How can they possibly do this, I hear you ask? It's really quite easy; the perpetrator can restrict access to transport to be able to get to a job by not allowing you to use the car or to allow you money for using public transport like the bus. A firm favourite with perpetrators as well is to turn off the alarm for the morning to make him late, I mean think about it, if you were an employer, would you tolerate someone that kept being late? In some cases, they will encourage their partners to take another job, or in some cases what can be more hazardous jobs that they know they will not enjoy, just because it pays more knowing that the likelihood is that they won't keep it. This opens them up to a large degree of emotional abuse around how they can't keep a job and that once again they're letting their family down.

Female perpetrators have also been known to harass their male victims whilst they're at work, constantly texting them all day and becoming abusive if they do not reply. One perpetrator cost her partner a job in quite a high-paid, respected position by constantly calling him or turning up at his office demanding he look after his child whilst she attends meetings or to do other things she needed to do (sometimes things like attending a session with a personal trainer). This progressed to her needing him to work at home more as she didn't trust the nanny that they had and once he did more days working from home, she was taking advantage of this to save more money by giving the nanny days off so he had to take charge of child care whilst he should be working, which led to him missing deadlines and ultimately losing his job.

Nearly all victims of abuse will experience economic abuse alongside other types of abuse; very few will say that it is the only type of abuse they are suffering. This type of abuse does so easily go hand in hand with other types of abuse. Many of those that do discover they are suffering from more types of abuse do so when they start talking about the issues they face. Economic abuse has a massive impact on male victims of abuse as it ultimately stops them from having money for the essentials they need within their lives. For those that have or are left with a debt as a result of abuse, they report that they do lose sleep sometimes more over the worry of the debt they are in rather than the abuse they are suffering, never knowing if they are going to get a knock on the door from a bailiff or to become homeless.

So why does the perpetrator do it alongside other types of abuse? Quite simply, it puts a barrier in place to stop their victim from being able to leave and also makes the victim dependent on them. And for those that do manage to leave? They still experience the implications after they leave as they quite often start again with no funds and a number of debts hanging over their heads.

Here in the UK, there are schemes in place for those that are on benefits, some of these may exist in other countries but we do not fully understand the measures each country offer. Below are some examples of support around benefits for those who are suffering from domestic abuse in the UK that may help:

Domestic Violence Easement:

For those claiming job seekers allowance or universal credit that have been subjected to domestic abuse in the last 6 months can be made exempt from certain work-related conditions that they usually need to meet (looking at the number of jobs they need to apply for or work-related skills courses they run).

Universal Credit Alternative Payment Arrangement:

Universal credit payments can be divided between partners in exceptional circumstances, including where there is domestic abuse (including financial abuse).

Obviously, they aren't just going to accept your word for the fact you are a victim of abuse, they need evidence of this that can be provided by someone supporting you in an official capacity due to the abuse. These are people like healthcare professionals, police or a domestic abuse worker. More details around this can be found on the gov.uk website.

Chapter Seven
The Use of Sex and Sexual Abuse

When we talk about sexual abuse and what behaviours constitute sexual abuse, the first and most obvious one that people think about is rape. But can a man be raped by a woman? According to what it says in the law within the UK, someone has been raped if:

"He intentionally penetrates the vagina, anus or mouth of another person with his penis without the consent of the other person and without a reasonable belief that that person has consented."

Firstly, notice that the definition starts with the word "he" and goes on to say with "his penis". So basically, the law states you have to have a penis in order to commit rape. However, a woman could be charged with the offence of assault by penetration if she uses a part of her body or another object to penetrate her male partner in a way that is sexual, non-consensual and without consent. The only other offence is that of sexual assault. The definition of sexual assault, which is what would logically be considered in most cases with a female perpetrator towards her male victim, is an act of physical, psychological and emotional violation in the form of a sexual act, inflicted on someone without their consent.

But it still is hard to find examples anywhere of females sexually assaulting men because the tactic she uses is that of coercion. This is what we aim to look at within this chapter.

Certainly, this was a subject that the majority of the men that I have worked with felt the most uncomfortable to talk about when this had happened to them. But the truth is, it does happen and maybe more commonly than we wish to consider. Female perpetrators can and do force, or a better word would be manipulating, their male victims into having sex when they don't want to. How do they do this? Well, in a variety of ways but the most common being guilt. By making their partner feel guilty, in some cases asking if they don't find them attractive anymore, the perpetrator can make threats to their victim about finding someone else that does want to have sex with them. They would point to co-workers, their boss, family members and even friends being who they were referring to. They can quite commonly use blame against the victim also, maybe by stating that there has got to be something wrong with them if they don't want to have sex. As we talked about in the earlier chapters, being made to feel guilty can often manipulate men into doing things that they don't want to do. They don't want to upset their partner so will have sex with them in an attempt to appease them. The same goes for being threatened and the blame game, men are manipulated into what it is their partner wants, in this case to have sex. Whilst we are looking at the topic of sex with other people, I have mentioned earlier in these pages about perpetrators cheating on their victims with others, this needs a mention again here as this can come with risks itself. There is always the possibility that the perpetrator could contract a sexually transmitted disease and their victims would know nothing about it, thus potentially being put at great risk.

One man that once shared his story with a few of us said that his partner had a thing about making him watch pornography with her and then making him re-enact what it is that they just watched. He said that he did it just to keep her happy as the first time she had tried it and when he had said no, she became verbally and then physically abusive towards him, using all the manipulation techniques that we have only just been looking at. He himself said he had no desire to watch porn and felt very uncomfortable with some of the things that she demanded he did, things like tying her down as he believed that she could turn that on him and use it against him with false accusations if she wanted to.

The ability to be able to use sex as a weapon is something that a female perpetrator has at her disposal to use against her partner, certainly as she will pretty much decide when and where they have sex. It certainly would not be unbelievable that she would withhold sex or any affection from him in the build up to an incident and then demand what is known as "make up" sex afterwards as a way of making up but, in fact, this is more about her having a way of keeping power and control over him. She can also use contraception, or the lack of it as a weapon, deciding if and when to use contraception, often not including him in the conversation. Certainly, this has happened in a number of cases that I have been involved in when the victim was making plans to flee the abuse. Who can say if she had found out in any of these cases or just if she just had a gut feeling something was happening but the perpetrator manipulates the contraception and the next thing the victim knew was that she was pregnant, which in most cases kept them within that abusive relationship longer.

Another thing that many don't consider, but can be used as a weapon against a victim, is revenge porn. This is perpetrated by both men and women but the cases with male victims are on the rise. Revenge porn for those that do not know, is the sharing of private sexual materials, be it video or photographs, of another without their consent, with the sole purpose of causing embarrassment or distress to them. One of the most common misconceptions though is that it has to be naked pictures or sex videos, but that is not the case at all, it can be someone posing in a sexually provocative way, lingerie shoots are now quite common with female victims of this crime. Now I've known this from two different situations, you can get the female perpetrator using pictures and videos as a threat to keep a man within the relationship or to use them against him if he leaves. I've had men explain how they have been threatened with explicit pictures and videos being posted on social media if they leave and I have been working with men that have fled where this has happened. The phrase comes to mind "hell hath no fury like a woman scorned" and that is certainly the case with our female perpetrator.

As I briefly looked at within the emotional abuse section, female perpetrators will also use sex as a weapon to be able to put their partner down, to refer to him as not coming up to the mark when it comes to being a "real man". This is done purely and simply to humiliate and reduce his self-esteem. The most common insult being that of "Is that it?" and passing judgement on him being rubbish and a waste of time. Usually, they would then use this against their partner on future occasions making comments like "After last time? Why would I want to have sex with you?"

So just why is it that men have difficulty in coming forward to report incidents of sexual abuse? Fear plays a big part in this, fear that they won't be believed if they try to tell someone. Embarrassment and shame also play a big role in preventing men from reporting too as many in society do not believe that it happens. There are plenty that pass judgement when it comes to sex and domestic abuse, that men cannot be forced to do anything they don't want to do. One man in a group once said "It was hard enough to speak out about the fact that I was a victim of domestic abuse, let alone speaking out about being sexually abused."

People's perceptions do need to be challenged around this issue as they do present a major barrier preventing male victims from coming forward. In stories that have been online where men have been sexually abused, there have been plenty of comments making light of the situation. One story I read was of a gentleman who when passed out drunk was put in the back of a car by an older woman who then proceeded to have sex with him. Some of his friends had watched this happen and nobody stopped it. When he asked some of them what happened, they had laughed and claimed that she had totally "raped" him. How is this funny at all? Let's take this story back to the start and make it a young woman passed out drunk that is put into a car by an older man. Suddenly, it isn't a laughing matter, is it? So why should it be with a male victim?

Ultimately male or female victim, no means no, anything other than this is a crime and victims of this type of behaviour should feel able to speak out. If you yourself have been a victim, don't suffer in silence, speak out to agencies that can give you the right help and support you in your decisions to move forward, catering to your individual needs.

Chapter Eight
Creating and Using Isolation

Isolation and domestic abuse go hand in hand; there is no way that the two can be separated in any abusive relationship. Isolation is one of the most powerful tactics that a perpetrator can use and it is one of the most commonly used. It is what the perpetrator does to convince their victim that they are the most important person in the world and the only one that they can rely on. By using this tactic, the perpetrator manipulates in a way that will cut their victim off from your family and friends, leaving them in full control of the relationship and more importantly to them, their life.

Why is this so important to them and why do they see this as something they simply need to do? This I will come on to, but first, let us have a look at some of the things that our female perpetrator will do to create the isolation. To effectively look at all areas that are affected when creating a state of isolation, I will break it down into four sections; friends, family, work and technology, remembering in each that the perpetrator's main aim is to control who their partner sees and what they do.

So, when it comes to the victim's friends, it will not just be close friends that have been around for some time, but social groups that they may well be involved in. Let's take football and rugby as these are two of the biggest sports we have in this country, and also the source of a number of incidents that I have come across. Most of these have started with the perpetrator questioning why their partner wants to go and play sports or as they put it, "kick a bag of air" when they could be spending time with them? One male that I worked with indicated that this had happened to him but it wasn't something that he thought twice about. He said that his partner, whom he had only been with for a short period of time had said that she felt she was always put second after his team mates as he worked long hours all week and then spent over half of his weekend, which is the time they should spend together, with his mates. He said that at the time he thought that her argument had some justification about it so he had hung his boots up and left his team at the end of the season to do just what she wanted, to spend all his time outside work with her.

For those that don't buy into this initially and don't just give up what they are doing, the perpetrator will attempt to start going everywhere with them as they want to be the centre of their victim's attention. And I mean everywhere. Again, let us take the sports match, they will start going to every game but make it clear that this is not something that they enjoy, but something that is expected of them. They will find anything and everything to moan about; in winter, for example, that it was cold and that she was frozen stood there watching him run about, or maybe that his team mates gave her the creeps the way they kept looking at her or even flirted with her. It is without question that this will start an internal war within their partner's mind as on one hand they will have been friends with their team mates for some time but will also want to believe their partner as they love them. It's a really difficult position for anyone to be in. Any attempts to defuse the situation with the perpetrator will be met with arguments such as "I knew it; I knew you would side with them. You always put them first."

This behaviour will be worse if the victim suggests going on a night out with their friends as the perpetrator will probably say in the first incidence that this is fine but go on to sulk and cause an atmosphere. I know many of you that have experienced abuse will know what I speak of next when I say that when you ask the question "what's wrong?", that is the chance that the perpetrator has been looking for to start an argument in an attempt to get their victim to stay home. Probably the most common argument will be that they trust their partner, but they don't trust their friends as they know what they are like, pointing back to how they have flirted with her in the past. It is also possible that she may try a different approach to this and try to entice their partner to stay home by either walking around naked or in seductive underwear; this in an attempt to show them what they're missing by going out. Some will go even further than this by insisting on them having sex before they go. Again, coercive ways to keep their partner home and begin to isolate them from their friends. Don't misread what I'm talking about here; I'm not talking about once in a while, this sort of behaviour happening most times.

It is a sure-fire guarantee that for those that are in these situations and do go out, they will be called and texted constantly throughout the night by their partner, checking up on them, wanting to know where they are and, who they've been spending time with. Does this ring a bell with any of you? It is possible that in an attempt to entice them home, they may follow up on earlier behaviour and start sending explicit text messages and picture messages also. From having witnessed this happen myself, I can say that when a male is out with his mates and his partner constantly calls, it will ruin his night out as he isn't able to spend time to relax with his friends and will feel that he should have just stayed at home in the first place. Not only that, his friends will also become increasingly annoyed as he is constantly on his phone.

I have also met a number of males that this has happened to, whose partners would use video calls through various apps and demand that they show them where they are and who they are there with as they claim that they don't believe they are where they say they are. One case in particular said that his partner would do this on the hour, every hour, as she wanted to make sure he wasn't in a gentleman's clubs with his friends as the only woman he should be looking at is her. This behaviour would annoy his friends to the point that they just stopped inviting him out.

A number of you may already be familiar with this but there was once a story that I read in the national papers of a male whose partner made him a t-shirt with a picture of them both and the words "I love my girlfriend and I hate all the girls in Ibiza so please stay away from me" printed on it and would make him wear it when he went out on nights out whilst on holiday with his friends, making him send photos so she could make sure he was wearing it. What was most shocking about this story was that the paper reported on this in a comedic way, referencing how he found it a bit of a laugh, not sure I or many others see it that way. Would it be seen as a laugh if it was the other way around?

Anyhow, I digress from what we were looking at. If these behaviours don't cause a separation between their partner and his friends, the perpetrator would employ different tactics to try and cause a problem in the relationships with his friends such as spreading lies about the friend. This causes a problem as when these friends would speak to our victim about this, the perpetrator would then deny that they had said anything, again pointing to the fact that his friends have never liked her. She will also spread lies about the victim to his friends too in an attempt to force an argument or rift between them. I have seen this happen once in my life when in a sports team I played in where the captain confronted another of the players about things he had apparently been saying, bad mouthing his ability as a captain and a player, which ended in the player being thrown out of the club even though the player denied saying anything. I was told by the captain that the player's partner had been saying things to his wife and that this is where the information had come from. I'd never considered before that perhaps this player himself had been a victim of abuse and that this was his partner trying to isolate him until now, when this example entered my head writing this.

Finally, one other thing that she will do is go out of her way to make the friends feel uncomfortable when they come into the home, maybe by slamming doors or walking from the room without saying anything, generally use her demeanour in an attempt to stop the friends coming back to the property again in the future.

This then gives you an idea of the sorts of behaviours that you may come across from a female perpetrator when trying to isolate their partner from his friends. But what about his family, these are people that have been part of their partner's life for a very long time. How does she go about trying to cause isolation from them? Surely these are bonds that are unbreakable.

It is my belief that the most common way that this starts will be that the perpetrator will claim that the victim's mother doesn't like them, that she has made it clear to her that she will never be good enough for her son. This will be denied by the victim, defending his mother at the start, but the perpetrator will start to engineer situations that she can then use to form doubt in his mind. This will continue over a period of time and the perpetrator will find ways to cause arguments with family members, usually by disagreeing with points of view in conversation or by being ignorant towards them. Sometimes these incidents will happen in plain sight and will make the victim feel very uncomfortable as they will feel that they have to take sides, but there will be other incidents going on when they are not around and all they will become aware of is the "atmosphere" that is within the room. Being a family-orientated person myself, I know that my family like to help each other out, isn't that what families do, but a perpetrator will make comments to their partner that it is just them interfering, sticking their nose in and it is his family trying to control what they are doing. Over time and with these events becoming common-place, the perpetrator will be continuing to make comments to our victim that they have never truly been accepted.

I remember from my early days of working within domestic abuse that one male that I worked with used to have a really close relationship with his mother which was broken by his partner's lies around birthday cards. It was an incident on his mother's 60th birthday where he had been snowed under at work and one evening just before her birthday, he had come home and said he needed to go out to get her a card. His partner told him not to worry as she had already got one and had dropped it around earlier that day. He was very thankful to her for this so imagine his shock when his father called him on the afternoon of his mother's birthday claiming that he had neglected to remember it. This caused a big heated argument which resulted in his dad slamming the phone down on him, saying he was a disappointment. He spoke to his partner about it when he returned home and she maintained she had given the card to his mother in person and that this was clearly just another way to try and break them up.

It is surprisingly quite a common occurrence for a female perpetrator to make accusations against their partner's male relatives, predominantly their brothers that they have made inappropriate comments to them or even gone as far as having tried it on with them. These types of accusation can break very close relationships to a point they cannot be repaired, as the confrontations after these accusations can flair up into physical altercations and see family members actually come to blows. Naturally, they will strongly deny what they are accused of and in turn point the finger of blame at the partner for being a liar. The result of this is as our victim loves their partner, they will be in a position where they have to defend them. As you can see from this example, it can and does create a real mess in these family relationships.

The fallout from these types of incidents can be felt by everyone. The perpetrator will refuse to have anything to do with their victim's family at all and will make excuses for not seeing them. She may also insist on them moving a little further away as she is feeling upset and stressed from the situation, also insisting that he doesn't tell them the new address as she doesn't want the issues following there.

Talking of housing, in other situations I have come across, the perpetrator has taken the responsibility of applying for housing through the council and has deliberately decided on a property that is in another area away from their partner's family and friends, stating it was all there was that was suitable. Obviously, as can be expected, this then pulls the victim away from the family and further into isolation and ultimately dependence on the perpetrator.

So now that we have looked at how male victims are isolated from their friends and family, let's take a look at how they are isolated from work and their colleagues there. Now I ask this question directly to you, do you work long hours and try to go the extra mile to stay secure in your job and help out your colleagues? How does your partner feel about this, is she supportive or does she criticise you for doing it despite the fact you bring home extra money? For a female perpetrator, their victim putting in long hours at work is like a red rag to a bull, it is not something she is willing to put up with even if it means extra money in the house. She will do all she can to stop him doing this, she will create rows when he gets back from work late (this is something that was portrayed well in a short film I saw as despite knowing her partner would be late back, a female perpetrator made him dinner early and made him eat a cold meal in front of her calling him ungrateful) and has been known to alter the clocks or switch off alarms so he is late to work in the first place. To us, it makes no sense, as for most of the men I know, myself included, we are working to make a better life for us and our families.

Jealousy of female colleagues also plays a prominent role; comments like "who is she?" or "how old is she?" are often heard by male victims accompanied by the desire for their male partner to change jobs and move to something in an industry that is a little less female-dominated or even better to have a job where it is possible to work from home. Because of the jealousy she will not like her partner to be going out on work night outs and will insist on attending any social or work events with him. There was one incident where a quite successful male client that I was working with had to attend a social event that was put on to celebrate a major contract that the company had secured, which he had to attend as he was the assistant on the project. His partner came along with him as she wanted to be introduced to his colleagues and, or so she claimed, to support him. On arrival, she was introduced to his boss, who happened to be female and immediately became stand-offish with everyone. When he asked if there was a problem, she immediately stated that she was not stupid and she accused him of working long hours as he was clearly having an affair with his boss. He denied this as he stated there was nothing but a professional relationship but her rationale was that he was a man, his boss was attractive and all men think with their dicks. What made the situation even worse was that his boss tried to engage her in conversation and she just ignored her and walked away. His partner became gradually angrier and later in the evening interrupted a speech his boss was making to publicly accuse her of sleeping with her partner. This outburst led to him losing his job as this had been done in front of major contributors on the project.

When there are children within the relationship, the female perpetrator will also use the children to influence his work choice. She will show up at his work place with the children claiming she cannot cope or constantly call him claiming to need him at home, all in an attempt to bring him away from work. It can sound quite farfetched some of the things written here in this section, but I guarantee you, each and every one has happened.

Here is the story of how one male that I worked intensively with lost his job in a very lucrative career that he had worked hard within for years. See, this gentleman (I call him this, as he was to every extent a real true gentleman) and his partner both worked, they worked really hard before the birth of their son. They were both very successful but his partner gave up her role in education to raise their son, which she had claimed she was more than happy with. Once he returned to work, he regularly got tearful calls from his partner claiming that she couldn't cope with everything that needed doing and looking after the baby. He explained that on a number of occasions, she turned up at his office and dropped the baby with him at work so she could get some alone time. He looked into an answer for this and decided with his partner to rearrange their finances and employ a nanny to help out with things around the house. Initially, this worked well and it came to a point where his partner also looked to return to her education role. Within the first week of this happening, he received a call from home to tell him that the nanny hadn't arrived so he needed to come home to have their son as she had responsibility for a number of children at work. He took emergency leave and later that evening they discussed what needed to be done and his partner asked about him working part-time from the home address so as he was there some of the time if needed.

Luckily, his work was quite understanding and implemented a home working schedule to allow him to work two days a week from home. Unfortunately for him, this move was the beginning of the end of his career as he was constantly being disturbed at home and a major assignment that he was working on was mysteriously deleted from his laptop. His bosses decided that he had become a liability and relieved him of his post within the company.

All of these sections here, friends, family and employment, all come together hand in hand and will not happen overnight. The three are a slow gradual process that happens together and without realisation most of the time, the male victim will not become aware until it has happened. It is a matter of manipulation so as she becomes the only person that the man has left in his life.

There is one more thing for us to look at when it comes to isolation and that is technology, which does need to be acknowledged as it is more and more frequently used. Most people these days are part of the "matrix" and use social media on several different platforms. Our female perpetrator will have the passwords for these as she will have demanded them due to a lack of trust over what he is doing on there, probably using the good old phrase "you wouldn't have an issue with it if you had nothing to hide". This leads to her looking through friends list, messages, emails, you name it, and she's looked. Then comes the questioning over "who's that?" and "you two seem overly friendly" and insinuating all sorts of things going on behind her back. She will also use his social media to send messages to different people pretending to be him. On Abused by my Girlfriend, Alex Skeel's mother received messages that looked like they were from him, telling her to stay away from them which she believed weren't from him, although at the time she couldn't prove it. This is common practice and too many men than I can count have reported the same sort of thing happening to them.

They will also conduct checks of text messages and call logs on their male victim's mobile phones to see who they have been talking to and what they have been talking about. They will also use their mobile phones to track where they are going, yes this is easier to do than you imagine. It is quite simple to link your iPhone to an iPad without the owner of the phone knowing about it and then they can see by download everywhere you have been and everything else. It's a scary thought, isn't it? Imagine what that is like if you are a victim of abuse and receiving support and all of a sudden you partner turns up where you are meeting the service supporting you. I've been on the end of a perpetrator turning up when conducting an appointment and it isn't something I would like to experience again. Certainly, if you have concerns about tracking devices through your mobile, take a look at one of the several videos available on YouTube that will talk you through the process of ensuring that it is turned off.

So, there you have it, she has successfully isolated him from these three groups, then to compound that isolation as he is not working, she will surely give him lists of tasks that she wants him to complete around the home (usually more than is physically manageable) to make sure that he doesn't have time to leave the house. She will also deny her victim access to transport or funds to pay for public transport as he in her opinion, he has nowhere he needs to go or in some cases, actually locking him in the home. Her claim though isn't that she is trying to keep him in but that she doesn't like it unlocked when she isn't there. The only time she will be happy for her victim to be allowed to go out or to use of the car is when it is to do something for her, and even then, she will always check the Satnav and mileage to see exactly where he has been.

So why does she do it? I'll tell you another story to fully explain. I had a client who met their perpetrator on a dating website and after meeting a few times and talking constantly, they decided to make a go of things. Now he was and always had been quite a social person, working in finance and spending most evenings after work chatting to his mates in the pub. He was also very close to his family, mum, dad, two brothers and a sister that he saw or spoke to most weeks.

The biggest issue with this new relationship was that even though she spent periods of time here, she lived in Paris and to try and get past this, she invited him to move in with her there when her current contract ended. Paris, the most romantic city in the world, who wouldn't? The problem was there were a number of things he hadn't considered. When he got there, most of the people he met did not speak a word of English which was an issue as he didn't speak a word of French. This meant that a once-social person became quite isolated and the only person he had to spend time with was his partner. This lack of being able to speak the language also impacted his career as he was unable to find suitable work, becoming financially dependent on his partner. The only thing he did have left was the weekly telephone contact he had with his parents until one day, he returned home and the phone line had been disconnected. When he asked why this was, she was quite abusive and said that she couldn't afford the constant calls to the UK when he wasn't contributing. It was from this point in she became emotionally abusive, calling him useless and other names and physically violent when she had been drinking (which was quite a common occurrence), when he told her what she was doing was unfair, she responded that his behaviour and reliance on her was unfair and he was greeted with what to me is the most emotionally abusive phrase there is, "man up" implying that he is not behaving like a man should.

I asked him why he thought she had done this and he was unsure. I explained to him that she had effectively isolated him from every person in his life. He had his friends that he used to drink with, they were now gone and all he had was her. He had his work colleagues; they were now gone and he was dependent on her. He had his family; they were now gone as he had no means of contacting them. I asked him who he had, and his response was just her, I asked when the abuse started, and he said he started recognising it more after he lost contact with his family. The final question I asked him was who was there that he could talk to about the abuse. Need I tell you his response?

The truth is that the female perpetrator will endeavour to isolate their victim from everyone so as they have nobody to turn to about the abuse they are suffering. It is a clever tactic that is used in nearly every case of domestic abuse that I have worked on. By doing this, the abuse will continue for longer periods of time as they believe that they can get away with it. The results of this on the victim is that they end up just doing what they are told to do as they have no other options, they have become dependent on her. If you feel this is happening to you, the most important thing for you to do is to talk to somebody. If safe to do so, there are a number of agencies that can be found via the internet who can offer support. Pick up the phone, talk to someone and gain some advice. It's not selfish, you won't be judged.

Chapter Nine
The Impact on and
Use of Children

This for me has been possibly the hardest chapter to write. This is because I have seen first-hand during my work the effects on the children of domestic abuse and also how they have been used as a weapon against male victims. The impact of not being allowed any contact with their children has destroyed the lives of several males that I have worked with and there is definitely a direct link between this issue and suicide.

I want to approach this chapter from both sides, starting with looking at the effects of domestic abuse on children within the home. Domestic abuse forms part of what has historically known as the toxic trio, the others being substance misuse and mental health. Where there is one of these, you can usually find one if not both of the others and the presence of the toxic trio has been found to increase the risk to children within the home.

From my experience of working within domestic abuse, it is a common belief for some that if the abuse does not happen in front of the children, they are not affected by it. The truth is that even though in some cases they may not see it, they will almost certainly be aware of the abuse and it needs to be remembered that it takes on more forms than just physical. Take away the physical aspects and there is still a chance that the children will see injuries caused by incidents, see broken furniture, smashed windows and holes that the perpetrator has put in doors or wall (yes, female perpetrators do this also). Children can also get caught in the crossfire of the incident and end up being hurt or seriously injured trying to protect the abused parent.

One thing that I used to always ask victims that I supported to consider, is that the children may not see what is happening but they can certainly hear it if there is shouting and objects being smashed or broken. I remember a situation where the victim we were assessing said just what I have been describing above, that the children are never present when the incidents were taking place. It was at this point my senses were heightened so to speak as I saw a shadow pass by the kitchen door. I asked if there was anyone else within the house and the victim said that they were alone. After telling them what I had observed, they opened the kitchen door and their 12-year-old son was still in the kitchen and hadn't gone to school as they thought. After he had left the home, I raised the point with the victim that he hadn't known that their son was there and could it be a possibility that this could have been the case at times of abuse also?

Any children within the home when there is domestic abuse will be suffering some form of emotional abuse without exception and are considered to be at risk of significant harm. If the police are ever called to an incident of domestic abuse within a home with children, they have a duty to inform social services, as this in itself is now classified as a child protection concern in its own right, and the safety of the children is of paramount importance as well as that of the victim.

For all children, it is upsetting to see or hear one of their parents being abused and this can be exhibited in different behaviours from different ages of children. Young children will become very anxious, start waking at night having had nightmares and may start to wet the bed when this hasn't previously been an issue. They may appear to be tired a lot of the time due to the difficulty they are experiencing sleeping, this sometimes caused by fear of what might happen to them or the abused parent, and one noticeable thing will be that they will start to exhibit temper tantrums. One thing that is quite common is not wanting to separate from the abused parent, when they are taken to school or nursery, crying and not wanting to let go of their parent.

Older children, however, react to domestic abuse differently, with boys and girls exhibiting different behaviours. Boys on the whole seem to express their feelings in an outward way by becoming aggressive or disobedient. It is common that they will use violence as a way to try and solve problems as this is what they have seen at home. It would not be beyond the realms of possibility for them to be in trouble at school for bullying or fighting with others; furthermore, their school work may also start to suffer (it would be hard to imagine that it wouldn't). Older boys may start to skip school, opting to play truant and to start using substances or self-harming as a way of blocking out disturbing experiences from home.

Girls on the other hand tend to hide their feelings, becoming more withdrawn from others and they may also start to show signs of anxiety and depression. Certainly, girls that experience domestic abuse within the home are statistically more likely to develop eating disorders and to self-harm by cutting or overdosing.

No matter the gender of the child, one thing that they do share is the fear of what might happen next and because of this, they try to anticipate what the perpetrator's next move may be, often blaming themselves when the next incident takes place.

So, what about the long-term futures of children that grow up with domestic abuse? It is said that children who live with domestic abuse are more likely to become involved in an abusive relationship themselves; some believe that this is because children do tend to copy the behaviour of their parents. Girls that see their mother being abusive may believe that this is how they should behave and boys may believe that abuse is just something that has to be put up with.

However, it is not always the case that the behaviours repeat. In a large number of cases, children don't like what they see when they are growing up and try their hardest not to make the same mistakes their parents did and try not to copy those behaviours they grew up with. They can still, however, be affected with mental health problems such as anxiety and depression and maybe other forms of post-traumatic stress disorder due to the environment they were subjected to during their younger lives. Without going into detail as it is very personal to my family, we suffered as children to abuse and some of us went on to experience abusive relationships. However, I can say that those of us that have learnt from our experiences and have moved on to have loving relationships, children of our own and a whole host of successes. This in itself shows that a child experiencing abuse can go on to live a happy, fulfilling life and isn't doomed to a life of misery and abuse.

Having looked at how domestic abuse affects children, let's now move on to look at how children are used to perpetrate abuse against their father, the male victim. There are a large number of tactics that a female perpetrator will employ involving the children to hurt and humiliate their partner or to try and keep or pull the male victim back into the relationship. It is also important to point out that in some cases, the female perpetrator may not even be the children's biological mother yet still use the children against the father.

One of the most common tactics that seemed to link a number of the fathers that I used to work with was that their partners would undermine them to the children, mostly by going against their instructions. Two of the most common examples of this was their father telling them that they couldn't have things and his partner giving it to them behind his back, the second is being told that they had to go to bed early only for them to be allowed to stay up late. One of the men that I used to support worked as a chef and had a real thing for making sure his children ate balanced healthy meals which I think is to be applauded, he did, however, have the same problems that most parents have and they certainly didn't always want to eat what he made. His partner, instead of supporting him and trying to encourage eating what had been made, told the children that they didn't have to eat it as they wouldn't be left to go hungry and that their dad would end up giving them what they wanted.

By doing this, what she is doing is trying to, and in most cases succeeding to do, is win their affection so as she can use them to perpetrate abuse against their father. Other ways that she will do this is by buying gifts or arranging to take them on days out, arranged on days that their father won't be able to come on due to work commitments. In some cases that I have worked, she has also put them down by calling them names in front of the children in a jokey way, encouraging them to join in with this. This can get extreme in very volatile situations and the name-calling can escalate. After separating from his abusive partner, a friend of mine told me that his ex was calling him a wanker in front of his children which was starting to be repeated on occasion. At the time, I couldn't imagine how that would feel, now having children of my own it is easy to imagine how it would feel if I was ever in this situation. My heart sank for him the one day we had been out for coffee; he was due to meet his ex to pick up his children to spend some time with them. When we left and he waited to meet his children, he was greeted by his son saying "Hello, wanker." This I heard myself and it was one of the most heart-wrenching things I had ever heard.

As I hinted at a short while ago, the female perpetrator will do certain things using the children in an aim to keep their victim with them. She could approach this from opposite angles; she could say that she can't cope without him and that the children may suffer because of this. This plays on the emotions of their father as he would not wish his children to suffer in any way, especially as it is a guarantee that she would not let him leave the relationship with his children. She will also use the children to isolate their male victim by stopping him from going out to see his friends, stating that if he rather sees his friends, then it's clear he doesn't really care about his children. Nine times out of ten this will be done in front of the children, further undermining the relationship with them.

The legal system is something she will try and use to her advantage, one thing she will certainly tell him is that if they separate, she will have custody of the children as they are always given to the mum and that she will do anything that she can to stop him seeing his children. She could also threaten any range of things from spreading rumours that the children seem scared of him when they are together or to make allegations that the children have said that he has done things.

I can remember a situation where one father I was working with had his children taken and given to the mother due to an accusation of emotional and physical abuse against his teenage daughter. It was alleged that he had shouted at her and intimidated her for taking items that he had bought for her to her mother's house and leaving them there and that he shook her when he was shouting at her. Obviously, I wasn't there but from what I had witnessed of him with his children, he would never raise his voice let alone ever physically touch them in any way. The issue he had was that he was a fighter as a career and it is my belief that that went against him with the allegations of physical abuse.

If our female perpetrator feels that she has lost her control over her victim, she will keep the children with her at all times to ensure that he cannot take them from her, this is sometimes enough to succeed in keeping her victim within the relationship. She will also use her emotions in front of the children to try and turn them against their father by making claims that he is leaving all of them. Can you imagine how that would feel to a child to be told a parent that they love and adore is leaving them? Additionally, how it would feel to be the parent of those children looking at you in that hurt and confused way?

It's difficult to read some of the experiences that are in here, isn't it? I assure you it is difficult to be putting these down in this book and reliving some of those experiences again. These were all difficult enough to go through with the victims but I have had reports of worse, lucky only once but once was more than enough as it was a case that had been taken further and reported to social services by the victim himself. In this case, the female perpetrator was extremely physically abusive towards him and had told him that he had experienced what she could do and could he imagine what she could do to their children if he left. By reporting this, it started an investigation and she was removed from the home and stopped from having any unsupervised contact. So, as you see, things don't always go against the father.

Female perpetrators will also use the children to emotionally abuse the father by questioning the paternity of the child. This is again something that I have had a lot of dealings with in my time supporting male victims. These experiences have seen multiple fathers be told that they are bad fathers and they will make statements about the children not really being theirs, in most cases this is not the truth and what she says changes when it suits her. It is said so as to cause hurt to their male victims, hurt that is amplified, as there is now that seed of doubt planted within their mind, where they just want to know if it is true or not. I cannot think of a worse thing that can be said to a man who is emotionally connected to a child and has raised them since birth. It has been described by one as like having your reason for existing taken away from you.

The problem seems to be, and this does go for all victims of abuse, when there are children involved even after separation the abuse does not stop as there is always going to be that connection until the children are old enough to make up their own minds. After separation, the continuation of the abuse will be felt for years. The female perpetrator may quiz the children to find out details about their victim, what they are doing now or if they are seeing anyone new, literally anything that they can find out that they can then use against them. She will then use this information to stop contact, forcing the victim to take things through the courts time and time again. The potential new relationship is one that comes up again and again with the contact being stopped as she doesn't know anything about this new person that is involved with HER children. The new relationship actually has nothing to do with it, it is just another way to hurt their victim by controlling them and dictating that the new partner cannot be around when the children are there or even as I have seen myself that all contact has to take place when she is there to ensure the new partner isn't. If the perpetrator gets a new partner, however, the rules change in an instant. She can and will use this new relationship to emasculate her victim and will praise this new partner in front of the children. Her new partner is never considered to be risk to the children in her eyes and she would be offended at the very suggestion that her taste in men was dangerous.

Using the courts to try and maintain a level of power and control over their victim is something that our female perpetrator will have no issue in doing and I have seen some shocking performances by them in courts myself when I have attended as a McKenzie friend (more of a moral support that can give the victim advice, but not address the court directly). The experience I would like to share feeds nicely into the tactic I was talking about above, when she uses her new partner to try and intimidate her victim. I attended court with one male that I had been working with for some time and on arriving in the court we were greeted in the waiting area by his ex-partner and her new partner. She spent the first 5 minutes sat there staring at us with a look of anger and her new partner stood up, crossed his arms and glared at me. Was I bothered? I actually found it childish and recommended to my client that we move to the opposite end, which we did. Eventually, we were called into court and we made our way in, getting comfortable and making sure we were ready. It was confusing why his ex-partner hadn't yet come in but then the court usher entered and spoke to the secretary, who in turn addressed the judges in this case to say that there was an order against my client and that she felt intimidated about coming into court alone and requested that her new partner be allowed to come in. This request was granted and she entered the court, looking scared and crying, and the complete opposite to what we experienced on arrival to the court. The aim was to win the court over to her side and have them looking at the actual victim in a negative manner.

When courts grant contact with the children, it is almost a certainty that she will refuse to help with travel arrangements to allow the contact to take place with the children, and push for stipulations that she feels will make contact difficult to achieve. I have been in a case where the victim suggested multiple people that his ex-partner knew to supervise the initial contact sessions. These were all rejected by the perpetrator and she stated that the children's grandparents who lived over 200 miles away were the only people she would accept. Now the male victim voiced his concerns as they were in their late 60's, not in the best of health and he didn't deem it a suitable arrangement; however, when the court contacted them to ask their opinions, they agreed as they just wanted to help (which she was more than aware that they would do). Needless to say, this fell through a few weeks in as one of his parents was unwell and the process started all over again with the blame being pointed at him as it was his parents that broke the contact.

During more recent times, there has been a spike in contact cancellations due to the Coronavirus pandemic. Despite advice given by the government that contact should not be halted, I have had dealings in a number of cases where mothers have found excuses like exposure to the public through working in supermarkets, belief that numerous people were going to the home in breach of regulations or even false reports of showing symptoms to halt contact. What angers me is then evidence arising that the mother has been taking the child to a number of places and mixing with a number of other people. There needs to be much more guidance given and repercussions when this is done. False accusations definitely play a big part in the cancellation of contact agreement.

The children and contact will continue to be a source of harassment moving forward until the children are old enough to make their own decisions. Handovers are always a flash point for incidents happening with numerous men reporting that without fail, their ex-partner would block off their path away from handover until they had had their say and verbally abused them in any way that they can. She will also continuously call, claiming that it is to check up on the children but predominantly to dish out more verbal abuse to the father. It's a real shame that when the father doesn't have custody of the children, which seems to lean towards the majority of these cases, the small amount of time that they are given is ruined by abuse from their perpetrator and they believe that there is nothing that can be done about it. My advice was always to report it as she could be served with a harassment order to give some protection from the abuse.

How does this affect the male victim? The father of these children that has a right to be in his children's lives, and they have the right to have him in their lives. Children do not need to have both parents together, especially when the relationship is abusive, but when it seems the only way to see them is to be with their perpetrator, it is common that the victim will go back. The fear of false accusations is a very real experience that male victims do have to live with as sometimes these accusations are believed which can then see others that they are close to starting to doubt them. When they are believed, they can have a number of repercussions for the father as it can leave them labelled as being a bad father and having to attend parenting classes, especially if professionals believe he "let" abuse continue.

Having these types of things happening, leaves the victim living with feelings of guilt and fear, often remaining in the relationship as they feel that this is just the way things have to be if he wants to see or protect his children. This again, as stated right at the start of this book, is one of the main reason's men stay within abusive relationships.

Using children as tools or weapons is wrong, there has been a case recently where the father was awarded custody of the son, as the judge ruled in the father's favour as he was suffering emotional abuse with the mother persistently portraying him in a negative light and said that the son identified with these hateful feelings she was expressing towards his father and mirrored her opinions of him. I just wish there were more cases like this.

I would like to end this chapter by sharing a poem with you as it is one that really made me think when it comes to this issue. It is called children live what they learn and is by Dorothy Law Nolte.

If a child lives with criticism, they learn to condemn.
If a child lives with hostility, they learn to fight.
If a child lives with ridicule, they learn to feel shy.
If a child lives with shame, they learn to feel guilty.
If a child lives with tolerance, they learn to be patient.
If a child lives with encouragement, they learn confidence.
If a child lives with praise, they learn to appreciate.
If a child lives with fairness, they learn justice.
If a child lives with security, they learn to have faith.
If a child lives with approval, they learn to like themselves.
If a child lives with acceptance and friendship, they learn to find love in the world.

Chapter Ten
Substance Misuse and
Domestic Abuse

Having now worked myself in both domestic abuse and substance misuse services, it is very clear that the relationship between both is a very complex one. As mentioned in the previous chapter, these two make up two thirds of the toxic trio, the third being mental health. It doesn't take a rocket scientist to realise as well that when there is domestic abuse, it will have a detrimental effect on the mental health of the victim and of the children within that situation. This means two of the three are already present before we even look at substances.

A large number of perpetrators will blame substances for their behaviour, be it drugs or alcohol, this I do not agree with. I don't believe the substances themselves cause the abusive behaviour but they do go alongside it and often exacerbate the situation. The statistics when it comes to substances and domestic abuse do not lie, the home office reports that just under 50% of convicted domestic abuse perpetrators have a history of alcohol dependence and around 75% had consumed alcohol before the incident that led to the conviction. This shows how even though I had changed services from domestic abuse to substance misuse, it has been quite easy to keep my knowledge sharp with domestic abuse.

To effectively look at both sides of the equation though, you need to look at how the perpetrator uses substances themselves as we have briefly discussed above and as a way to control their victim, but also at the victim's use of substances as a way to cope with the abuse they suffer, as well as potential dependence.

If you go back to the start of the book where we looked at the power and control wheel, certainly on paper, looking at the different types of abuse and what has been included in the chapters so far, there were some shocking examples of what male victims have suffered at the hands of their perpetrators. Now take that incident, add alcohol to that mix, those behaviours or tactics under the influence of any substance can raise the risk levels massively (as the assault with the stiletto shoe showed, that so easily could have been another death statistic).

When we have major sporting events, there is always a massive promotion on domestic abuse as there is evidence of a spike in abusive incidents at these times. I don't disagree with this but what does get little promotion is that it isn't always men that get abusive during these tournaments. I know a great number of males that suffered at the hands of a female partner after their team has lost a major game. Also, men have been known to suffer abuse from their partners on returning home intoxicated from a day out with their friends where they have been watching the match. It is all too common a theme that on the surface it was alright for them to go out and enjoy themselves but on returning home, an incident ensues with arguments over the amount of time that they have been out and/or the amount of alcohol they have consumed. One male that I know personally was punched and slapped around the head when he got home at 8pm in the evening for wasting money on alcohol (that may I add he had earned) that could have been spent on other things, even though she had been fine about him going earlier in the day.

So, what about the victim and their use of substances and the impact on domestic abuse? I can say that a large number of victims of abuse that I have come into contact with will use drugs or alcohol as a way of coping with what is happening to them, with alcohol being the predominant substance due to the ease of availability. For those that suffer physical abuse, they openly say that it numbs the pain that they feel when they are assaulted which makes it easier to deal with. Men say that for the constant emotional abuse and threats that they face on a day-to-day basis, alcohol and drugs help them to block this out. Granted, many people may think that using substances is not a good way to cope with this, but for someone that is facing the same behaviours on a day-to-day basis, it becomes more about ways to survive, and if substances help them through this period, then who are we to judge? Domestic abuse is a massive trauma for anyone to suffer, and for trauma victims it is not uncommon for substances to become a coping strategy.

What may be even more concerning, is that some victims I have worked with have said that they will use alcohol as a way to gain the confidence to instigate the physical abuse that they know is coming their way so as they are not waiting and waiting for what they know is coming. I can understand this to some degree but wouldn't advise this as a course of action due to the increased risk that they would be placing themselves in as this tactic can escalate the situation even more.

Another course of action that I know that some victims have taken in the past is to buy their perpetrator more alcohol in an attempt to delay the abuse. This I know is difficult to get your head around but let me explain, it becomes clear quickly. Some victims reported that there were certain situations, like their partner going out with a certain group of friends that inevitably ends up with them coming home intoxicated and starting the abuse. But they discovered that by buying another bottle of wine and leaving it on view with a glass would lead to their partner drinking a little more and, in most cases, passing out, meaning that for that night the victim had pacified the abuse. Again, I'm not sure how I feel about this course of action but fully understand why they had decided to do it if, as they say, it stopped an incident of abuse.

So, knowing that victims also use substances predominantly as a way to cope, what other ways can a perpetrator use substance misuse to control a victim of abuse? There are several ways that I can think of and have also seen on a number of occasions. First, is that of forcing a partner to use drugs or alcohol. Not forcing as in injecting them directly, although I do know of at least one incident where a perpetrator had tried and forcibly injected their partner with heroin to cause addiction in hope that this will keep them in the relationship. I'm talking about supply and demand, they supply it and demand their victim use it as they become more compliant when they do or that they could introduce it as a fun thing to do, getting high together. I've known it on a couple of occasions where the victim has been introduced to a substance that is highly addictive, like heroin, which they have then become dependent on their perpetrator to supply. This gives an extreme amount of control to the perpetrator as they can then withhold the substance until their victim does whatever they want them to do.

The most disturbing incident that I have come across when working in domestic abuse was a female perpetrator buying drugs for her partner knowing that he was addicted and when presented with them and encouraged, he couldn't resist using them. She would then video him whilst intoxicated, show him the footage and threaten to use this as evidence against him to stop him seeing their children if he ever tried to leave. True to her word, when he left the relationship, these videos were given to the courts as a reason why she felt he was a risk to their children and contact outside of supervised contact was refused. Substances do pose a risk to children so this result was inevitable even if the full picture had been taken into account.

Ultimately, this is why substance services are well trained to understand and identify abuse due to the close connections between the two issues. They understand the role that substances play for both perpetrator and victim in domestic abuse situations and are able to support victims to access specialist services that can help. I know that my colleagues that I have worked with over the years do this on a nearly daily basis and are very good at what they do. So, if you recognise any of these situations in your own life, if substances are an issue for you as a result of domestic abuse, this does not make you a bad person, you've survived in the best way you knew how. Please don't be afraid to come forward and speak out. You're support sessions are designed to be a safe and confidential environment to speak and they can provide the tailored, individual support you potentially need to stay safe.

Chapter Eleven
Exploitation of Disabilities

Domestic abuse as we know from the estimated figures is occurring in the UK at an epidemic rate, with the figure now sitting at over 2 million per year. When it comes to people who have disabilities, they suffer higher rates of domestic abuse. Those that have what is described as a limiting disability (a disability that limits their ability to do day to day tasks) are over twice as likely to experience domestic abuse than those without disability. When it is estimated that one in five of our population has a disability, as you can imagine, that this could be a significant figure. The other thing to take into account is that victims with a disability are more likely to experience domestic abuse for much longer periods of time and on a more frequent basis. This could be perpetrated by their partner, family members and even personal care assistants believe it or not.

I hear some of you asking how this is possible. Surely, there is a greater protection in place for these more vulnerable people? Well actually it's because of that vulnerability that potentially their ability to defend themselves or to report the abuse is more limited, and escaping the abuse can be nigh on impossible. Add to that what we have spoken of earlier within this book that men just don't recognise abuse, well this is still the case for men with disabilities. Let's consider for one moment a male that is suffering from domestic abuse that is autistic, I myself have supported men that this would refer to. Having that inability to read people and situations would mean that they are unlikely to realise without interventions that some of the more subtle types of abuse are occurring. It's not easy to read and realise that this is actually happening for so many, let alone additionally vulnerable people I know.

But unfortunately, this is a reality for those that need the assistance with what we consider simple day to day activities, they come into contact with many more people that could certainly use coercive and controlling behaviour against them. This reliance on these individuals can certainly exacerbate the difficulties that they would face compared to able bodied victim to be able to leave an abusive situation and to access key services such as domestic abuse services or even the health and social care teams that are there to protect them.

As with the way this book has been laid out so far, I would like to look at some of the behaviours that a male with disabilities can be subjected to when abused by a perpetrator, specifically targeting their disability as a tool or focus point for the abuse. Please also remember that these behaviours are not limited to what is included in this chapter, there are probably many more that I have not encountered and these are on top of the abuse that we have already covered.

When we looked at abuse in the earlier chapters, one of the things that was covered was the name calling. The results of this on a continued basis day after day does have a serious detrimental effect on that person that is the target of the abuse. So how do you think this would affect a person with a disability if it was that disability that was the focus of the name calling? Having the need for assistance can be difficult enough to come to terms with but imagine the impact when the person who you rely on constantly calls you "useless" or "pathetic". One gentleman, and I refer to him in this way as he truly is a gentleman, that I have exchanged experiences with who himself is blind, once told me that his perpetrator used to constantly tell him that having to help him dress and all the other things she had to do for him was like "having another child" to look after. As if this wasn't bad enough, he clearly remembered a situation where he felt humiliated by her when they required a taxi to take them somewhere and she apologised to the taxi driver for the delay, it was because she had to get "him" ready, as though he wasn't even there. Now I know from the conversations that I have had that this type of incident seems to be a common place with victims who have a disability.

Now, another tactic that is employed and is a way of undermining their confidence, is to make them feel guilty for the support that they have to provide. Now is it just me, or would you do these things for someone you care about or someone that you agreed to care for? But this is real, perpetrators make a point of letting their victim know what they have missed out on by having to be there to attend their needs. The guilt this causes is one of the many reasons why male victims do not speak out, due to the guilt their perpetrator has subjected them to.

When you turn your attention to the more psychological abuse tactics used, isolation does play a key role as within all abusive relationships. For those that require assistance in being able to get anywhere, perpetrators will deny them transport to places they need to go unless they comply to the demands that they set them. When it comes to important appointments such as GP's or hospital specialists, the victim reluctantly will do this due to the need for their perpetrator's assistance. But when they get to these types of appointments, it is very unlikely that the perpetrator will allow them to go in unattended as is the way with anything involving any other professionals. This is common place with any victim of abuse but in the case of those with significant care needs, they may receive threats of being placed into a care home should they speak out meaning even more significant loss of freedom. The thing is that, as with all perpetrators, they can be very convincing and this means they are more often than not believed, certainly when these types of threats are made towards our disabled victims.

Now I have a few situations that I have become aware of over the years that sit between this category and potentially that of physical abuse as well. So, I have made the decision to write about them here before I move on to physical abuse.

When discussing the issue of disabilities and domestic abuse, I was made aware of a situation one man found himself in at the hands of his daughter. He was a wheelchair user but could get around with the use of crutches. I don't know the full ins and outs of the situation surrounding this incident, but ultimately this does not matter as her behaviour was inexcusable. She deliberately threw his crutches down the back garden and told him if he wanted them, he would have to fetch them himself, knowing full well that this was impossible and leaving him stuck in his wheelchair.

The second situation was that of a blind man whose perpetrator was his wife. On the one situation she left him deliberately stranded on a busy motorway slip road as she decided that she didn't want to guide him anymore. Both of these situations actually occurred and both could have had quite serious consequences for the victim.

The final one that I feel sits between the two categories is that of withholding medication. I say this sits between the two as it not only has the emotional impact on the victim but the potential serious physical implications or even death. For those that have an inability to reach higher up places, it is known that perpetrators will leave their victims medication in view but just out of reach before they leave the home. This means that the victim has to spend their time knowing that it is there but also knowing they have no way to get to them. Can you imagine how that must feel, certainly if they need this medication for a serious condition? And what of the perpetrator is ever questioned about this? Excuses that they forgot due to the amount that is required of them to do? That it was a simple mistake? And would they be questioned over it? Who knows?

But withholding medication is not the only thing that perpetrators will withhold from their victims. For those with disabilities that require assistance to prepare food and drinks, this is also used as a method of abuse. Making them wait for meals when they are hungry or skipping the meal altogether, the same goes for drinks. Another thing that I have had numerous reports of as a method of abuse is when a victim requires their perpetrator to help them eat or drink and they deliberately put these into their mouths when they are too hot. Again, cue the excuses of it being an accident due to the sheer number of tasks that they have to complete, even though it is simple a task to test the temperature of food and drink, I mean the majority of the time you can see steam rising from it. Okay granted, occasionally this may happen by accident, but in abusive situations this would happen on a frequent basis.

So, we've covered a number of tactics and behaviours that are done directly towards the victim due to their disability and it goes without saying that the types of abuse covered in the chapters around financial abuse and sexual abuse does also apply to this cohort of victims too. The conversations that I have held with victims that have suffered these types of abuse have been difficult to hear, having relatives that themselves have disabilities made this very close to home. I feel lucky that for me, these relatives are still independent and don't require the level of support that other do, meaning they would not face the situations discussed.

To end this chapter, I would like to make one point to anyone who finds themselves relating to what we have covered. Male adults with disabilities commonly accept abuse from their partners or carers because they are frightened of losing the carer / level of care required or ending up in a care facility away from friends, family and freedom. If this is you, please speak up at any opportunity as the reality is that this will not happen as there are many agencies out there that can supply carers to meet your needs.

Chapter Twelve
Dynamics of Abuse in a Same-Sex Relationship

Whilst much of the abuse that we have been looking at and describing in the previous chapters of this book has been focussing on female perpetrators of domestic abuse, many of the tactics described will be similar to that experienced by gay and bisexual men. They can also experience different types of abuse based on their sexuality. This in itself prompted me to include a short chapter devoted to looking at this issue.

Domestic abuse does not discriminate and effects every type of person from all cultures, ages, gender, sexual orientation or beliefs. There are a number of surveys out there that suggest that one in four men in same-sex relationships will experience some form of domestic abuse. That's certainly higher than the one in six men in heterosexual relationships. This figure, however, doesn't surprise me but in the years that I was supporting male victims, I only actually supported two men from same-sex relationships. This is a very small number if the one in four figure that is used is correct. The reality is that those involved in gay or bisexual relationships, and transgender men equally valid in these identities, are often afraid of revealing their sexual orientation and going into the nature of their relationships if they were to disclose the abuse that they suffered. Historically the experiences of the LGBT community have been rife with homophobia, biphobia and transphobia. Quite simply, it's a lack of understanding of these relationships and the dynamics that can result in a victim being highly vulnerable. As with all male victims, this results in under reporting of crime, crimes not being taken seriously or the death of the victim.

Alongside this, as with what I experienced within the male service on a day-to-day basis, abused men in same-sex relationships did not recognise the behaviours as abusive but as normal behaviour, which is hardly surprising when predominantly everything there is to read about domestic abuse indicates a female as the victim. There is a lot that can be read about what is a positive heterosexual relationship but there aren't the same "standards" out there regarding healthy same sex relationships. The introduction of Section 28 in the UK by Margaret Thatcher in 1988 was a key player in the suppression of gay identity and expression. A lack of representation of LGBT relationships within sexual education has created generations of internalised homophobia and lack of safe sexual practices which produced large numbers of deaths in the AIDS crisis, as well as a lacking in healthy relationship dynamics. During this time every member of the LGBT community was made to feel undesirable, unclean, disgusting and that something was inherently wrong with them. It is the belief of many that it was this that gave life to the unsafe practices of dogging (watching or engaging in sexual activity in a public place) and cottaging (engaging in homosexual acts in a public toilet). Even in the world of kink, the freedom of this sexual expression is tainted by a few perpetrators that inflict pain on their partners under the guise of kink but have no safe words, no concept of safety during more hardcore kinks such as breath play, as well as no aftercare practices which results in long term harm to their victim's mental state as well as the bruises and welts left behind.

Talking to one of the men that I did support, they did disclose that they found it difficult to come forward to ask for help for pretty much the same reasons other men did that had accessed the service I worked for. He felt that there weren't any services out there that would support him as a man, certainly as a gay man that limited his options further, that he wouldn't be believed over what was happening to him and how he was suffering and that he would be treated with contempt, not only as a male victim but also as a gay man. The reasons that gay men stay in an abusive relationship are again exactly the same as those reasons that heterosexual males stay in relationships too. Literally no difference as some of these men too had children. They also believe too that their partner will change and that they would promise to get help, also some believed that if they themselves change their behaviour then their partner will behave differently and as with other men, they stay because they love their partner.

There are many young men that also experience abuse from other family members whilst they are exploring their sexuality and discovering who they are, if they are going to come out as gay or bisexual. This comes with added dangers for recently out trans men, who come out as gay or bisexual, as family members, friends and colleagues could struggle to understand the concept. I have had conversations with male friends that are gay who struggled to come out to their families as they didn't know how they would react, as they didn't want to hurt their feelings. One also had the added issue of a certain family member who would continuously pass homophobic comments in the form of jokes. Add to that the fact that in certain cultures, even here within the UK, gay or bisexual relationships are frowned upon and can result in being outcast from the community and in worst cases being the victim of physical assault or death. This makes things a lot clearer about some of the difficulties gay men face in abusive relationships.

A perpetrator of abuse can use the fact that their victim is gay or bisexual to assert power and control over them. They could threaten to disclose their victim's sexual orientation without their consent to other family members, to employers, to sports clubs, to name just a few but the list is endless. If the victim isn't ready to disclose this, someone holding the threat of disclosure over their head can lead them to do anything that is asked of them to keep this information quiet. Following on closely to this, if the perpetrator is a partner, they may have not come out themselves yet and force their victim to remain silent and straight-acting, doing the same as them so as no one finds out about them until the perpetrator decides that they are ready, which may be never. This can lead to the victim feeling extremely isolated, anxious and invalidated, and has contributed to the already high LGBT suicide rates that we see in this country.

You do also have to look at and take into account transgender men in same-sex or even heterosexual relationships. As with gay men, being outed to their family is extremely detrimental, especially if the family has a lack of awareness or understanding. Transgender men also face abuse from their partners in the same way as any other men but also have to face the abuse that is specific to them. One of the most common is that of what is referred to as dead-naming which is basically calling them by their name that they used to use, this can cause a massive amount of emotional and psychological distress, as well as gender dysphoria. They can also be prevented from accessing healthcare needs that they have, unless they do certain "things" for their perpetrator. This can prevent them from access to necessary surgeries or even obtaining testosterone and other medications they may take for any condition.

Other behaviours that I have come across through different agencies when it comes to same-sex relationships are things like violating boundaries that have been set through behaviours towards the victim, ignoring safe words that have previously been agreed on and going past their limits during sexual intercourse. As with other abusive relationships, there has been use of pressurising or forcing to have sex or to have sex with others (in this case other men) and the pressure of using substances to help "get in the mood" or enhance the experience for sex with drugs (chemsex), alcohol or poppers.

Society itself also plays a big part. There is still a distinct homophobic presence in today's society and this can be held in part responsible for some of these relationships remaining secret. It is as though for some within the LGBT community, they see that society expects them to behave in a certain way (a bit like in the film "The Stepford Wives") and it has been this way for decades. They feel they have to behave in that way to set an example, even if it leads to abusive or destructive behaviours. Even agencies within society that are predominantly there to help people have a distinct lack of knowledge and understanding of the dynamics of a LGBT relationship which again leads to isolation and being "stuck" within that abusive relationship. For those that do want to leave, this can be difficult in itself due to the lack of dedicated refuge spaces for gay men within the UK.

Perpetrators of abuse within a gay or bisexual relationship will always try to convince that their abusive behaviour is normal for this type of relationship. When their victim is inexperienced in relationships this can be a very effective tactic hidden under the guise of kink or expectation due to "men being men". But as with any form of abuse, it is not normal in any relationship, including same-sex relationships. Abuse has no part in any healthy relationship no matter what the sexual orientation is. You have the right to be protected from domestic abuse in the same way anybody else does and there are a number of services that can give you advice and support, which you can also do anonymously. Within the next chapter we will look at how to stay safe in a relationship; this goes for any male victim regardless of their sexuality and identity.

Chapter Thirteen
A Guide on How to Stay Safe

When it comes to abusive relationships, the victim has no control over their partner's abuse, but there are things that you can do to reduce the potential for harm. My experience is that although it is impossible to remove the risks that are there until you have managed to get out of this situation, by doing some simple safety plans, you can successfully reduce the risks of harm that you face.

A safety plan is basically a tool that can help you to identify options that are open to you and decide which would be best for you. What is important, however, is that it is you, the victim, that makes the decisions on what is the right option for you, primarily as if you make your plan, you are more likely to remember it. Also, you know your home, area and your situation better than anybody else. What I hope to do in this chapter is to give you some valuable tips on things to think about within three different scenarios:

- Staying in the relationship
- Planning to leave
- After leaving

One of the most important things that you may want to consider putting together regardless of which of these situations applies to you is what I call a survival pack. I call it this as it is the things that you will need when you flee from your abuse and move from victim to survivor. So, what sort of things do you think you would need to include? Let's start with your basics:

- Clothes – you will want to make sure that you have at least a change of clothes for you and any children that you have.
- Bank card and money – goes without saying that these are necessities when fleeing as you won't get far without them.
- Identification, passports and birth certificates – you will certainly need any passports and birth certificates for children as you may need to apply to change benefits for them to come to you and without them it would prove difficult (although not impossible). Also, by having the children's passports it makes it impossible for your partner to leave the country with the children, which it saddens me to say; I have had to support someone around before now.
- Mobile phone and charger – having your mobile phone with you is important. Don't worry about calls from the perpetrator, these days you can block their number. It is important as it holds all your numbers, numbers that you may well need moving forward and numbers that you potentially wouldn't want them having (friends and family).

This covers your basics but there are also some less common things that you may want to think about, things like:

- Medication – not vitally important as I'm sure you could get this replaced quite quickly through your doctor but for some conditions this would be needed to possibly keep you alive so needs to be thought about.

- House keys – my advice is to always having a house key so as you have access back into the family home at a later date to be able to reclaim some of your belongings. Always do this with support though and never alone.

- Mortgage or rent statement – if you flee from the home address you will want to let them know what has happened as if your partner stops paying, if you are on the agreement, you still remain liable for the debt.

- Unpaid bills – you may think "is this really important?" but I think it absolutely is. If you are getting away for a new start there could be nothing worse than unpaid bills appearing out the woodwork. At least if you take them, you can make contact, make them aware of your situation and at least put some sort of payment plan in place whilst you settle. Most companies are really good with these sorts of situations and will even agree to hold your account for 28 days.

What you will also want to consider is where you would want to keep these items. Leaving them within the home can be very risky as if found by your partner, it will make the potential for harm escalate massively. You need to consider if there is a friend or family member that you can leave these items with, ensuring it is someone that you trust.

Staying in the Relationship

Let's start by looking at things that you can do if you are still in the abusive relationship to keep yourself safe. It seems the sensible place to start is at the point the abuse starts, when you're with your partner. The most important thing that I can advise you to think of to keep yourself safe (and children if this is the case) is to be ready to call 999 if the abuse is, or becomes physical and the need is there to. It is also important to ensure that you keep your mobile phone charged at all times. I hope it is never the case but this could be the difference between life and death. Here are some other pointers for things you may wish to consider:

- It is worth thinking about your surroundings when a volatile "incident" occurs. It makes sense to avoid high-risk areas such as the bathroom (only one way in or out) or the kitchen (far too many potential weapons to even go into). You should also as part of this plan, be looking at possible escape routes for this type of situation for when you may need them.
- Do you have a neighbour that you get on well with that you feel you can trust to make them aware of the situation? This can be very beneficial as you can then ask them to call the police if they see or hear anything suspicious. One of the safe houses that I used to help

manage (a one-bedroom flat) had a really nice neighbour who knew what we operated and always spoke to me when I was there to say that they would call the police if they were concerned.

- It is useful to have friends or family that you can call in an emergency (if you haven't been isolated from them). What I would advise is to have a code word that you create between you so they know that if it is used, that you are in trouble and you need help. This has saved so many victims over the years, both male and female, including two that I have worked with as using this code word prompted a safe and well check by the police which brought a potentially life-threatening incident to an end. This can also be useful for children so as they know that they need to leave the room that they are in when you suspect a volatile "incident" is forthcoming.

- Whilst we are talking about children, it is important for them to know what is happening if they are not too young and encourage them not to get involved as it poses a massive risk to them.

- Plan and choose somewhere that you will go in an emergency, be it a friend or family member, and plan the route you will take to get there.

- It is also important to consider keeping a log of all the incidents that are happening as this could be used at a later time when needed. You would need to include dates and times, what happened, injuries received, witnesses and if you saw any professionals as a result of this. This can be done via an app that can be downloaded to a mobile phone called Bright Sky.

- Sometimes, this isn't easy to do but you should consider putting safe small amounts of money over a period of time so as you have some should you need to leave. This can be difficult, especially if your partner controls the finances but even a small unnoticeable amount every so often is better than nothing.

When it comes to keeping records, I know that for a large number of victims they are just not ready to talk to the police or to do anything about their abuse. That's OK; you need to deal with these things in your own time. But in the UK, there is also a service called VEV (Visual Evidence for Victims). It does run in a number of areas across the country and details can usually be found through your local authority website.

VEV is a collection of approved agencies that can take photographs of injuries and damaged property for victims over the age of 18 and store them securely for up to 6 years to be used at a time when you are ready to take things further. This way none of the evidence of what the perpetrator has done is lost.

Planning on Leaving

This is the point where you have made that decision that enough is enough and you need to get out from where you are. This is also the riskiest point in terms of abuse and harm so it does take a lot of planning as a good exit plan can reduce these risks dramatically. If you feel able to, this would be a good time to speak to the police to make them aware of your situation and that you are planning to leave as they can offer support through this.

So, as with before, let me give you some things to consider when putting your plan in place:

- You remember the survivor's pack we were talking about at the start of this chapter? Well, it is a good idea to speak to the person who is holding this for you so as they are aware of your plans to leave. This ensures that you will have access to your items at the time you need them.
- You will need to consider where you will go to, be it a friend or family member, the reality is it isn't likely to be a refuge due to the lack of provision for male victims in any country.
- It is best to consider a time when your partner is not at home to leave as this reduces the risk of conflict. If, however, they do return when you are in the process do not hesitate to call 999.
- If you have children, this can be where things get a little trickier. It is best not to involve your children in the plan to flee as they could unintentionally tip off your partner by saying things. You may even want to consider taking legal advice in advance around the children as well and consider contacting the NCDV (National Centre for Domestic Violence) or approaching the courts yourself to take out a non-molestation order.

It is a big decision to make to leave the relationship and move into the unknown. I think one of the biggest misconceptions is that if you are a victim of abuse, you have to leave the area that you live in. Certainly, that seemed to be what local authority housing always used to say. That in itself is an amazing idea, you've just fled from a relationship where isolation was a big weapon against you and now you have to leave everything and everyone you know. So, in effect you've left isolation to move on to isolation, excellent thinking, isn't it? The truth is that housing providers have to support you if you wish to stay in the same area; there is nothing in housing law that says you have to leave your area. I think this is done because it is just an easier option; I have no evidence to back it up, just a gut feeling.

After Leaving

That's it; you've done it and been able to get away from the abuse. Job done, move on with your new life risk-free. Sadly, this is not the case, at least initially. Departing an abusive relationship is considered to be one of the most dangerous times for escalation and this includes the initial period after you have left. This risk is possibly greater if you have chosen to stay in the local area.

So, what sort of things should you be considering to keep yourself safe during this period?

- It may be worth considering adding additional locks to your property, window locks that work and a deadbolt on the front door are things I used to help clients to sort out. Also motion sensor lights for outside the property so you know if someone is approaching. This is something that can be funded via support services such as IDVA (Independent Domestic Violence Advisors).

- As before, keep a diary of events if you continue to be harassed by your ex-partner as this can help should you need to take further action. The police may consider putting a marker on your home that would indicate that you were at risk and if a call came in, it would flag up as a high-risk situation. They are called different things in different places but they are called gazetteer markers where I live.

- If there is any reason that you need to meet with your ex-partner (apart from around children I can't see any reason why there would need to be), it would be advisable to meet with them in public and not invite them your home, or go to theirs for that matter. If this cannot be avoided, my advice would be to have someone with you.

- If you have children, it is worth speaking with the school to make them aware of the situation and that the children are living with you. I have worked with a number of dads in this position and there has been incident where the children's mother has gone to the school to try and take them. The school on each occasion has contacted the dad and not let the children go until he has arrived so as to safeguard the children.

- Again, around children, any contact that is arranged as your ex-partner will be entitled to contact, unless she poses a risk to them, access should be considered through a third party. Family members and friends can pick them up and drop them off at pre-arranged points.

- If your ex-partner does start to appear around your place of employment, it is worth considering having a conversation with your boss around this. There are things that employers can do to ensure that they do their bit to keep you safe whilst at work.

One really important thing to say at this point, it takes great strength and self-control to put up with abuse for any period of time. Everyone has their breaking points but it is imperative that you don't retaliate. Any retaliation could see the tables turned and you charged as a perpetrator of abuse, especially if you cause injury. It does happen. I have spoken to a few men over the years that this has happened to where defending themselves caused injury to their partner, the results being a custodial sentence and a criminal record. What is a better option is to know the signs and triggers and try to remove yourself from the situation as best you can.

As you can see, there are a lot of things to think about when it comes to safety and domestic abuse, and all of this can seem quite daunting. But safety plans are effective and there are plenty of agencies and people out there that can help with this.

Police

Male victims of domestic abuse quite often feel that there is no point in calling the police as they do not think that they will be believed or that people will look down on them as being weak for being abused by a woman. But the truth is that the police do treat all incidents of domestic abuse as a high priority. I'm not saying that there haven't been issues regarding the police as I would be a liar to say so, but that is the same with some female victims.

Take a situation where over a period of years, a male victim has been abused by his partner which has resulted in the police being called due to it escalating to physical harm after having had a drink. When I say physical harm, I'm talking his shirt ripped off and nail marks on him, I'm talking a small counter top freezer being thrown at him, and I'm even talking to the point that a TV was smashed over his head. Yet, when the police attended, they always took him away from the property to a place of safety and never arrested her. What sort of message does that send to a perpetrator? I imagine it kind of makes them feel a little indestructible. Had it been the other way around, would they have done the same or would they have left the property with him in handcuffs? I know what my thoughts are on this.

There was yet another situation where there was an occupation order keeping the mother away from the home, which she breached by kicking in the door but because she co-owned the property, the police in attendance said there was nothing they could do as she took items away from the house.

Again, I reiterate that these sorts of incidents are rare, but do happen on occasion. I hear you ask "why then do I raise them if they are rare?" The reason I raise them is because even rare is one too many. The first story I told you could have so easily, on a number of occasions, ended with a death, and then the police held to account over their actions or lack of in this case. And that would be such a shame as they work hard doing what they do and do keep so many victims of abuse safe. Just to balance it up, there was a time that I was aware of, that the perpetrator was so confused to be told she was under arrest that she became abusive to the officers stating that they couldn't arrest her as they didn't have a female colleague there and if they touched her, she would make accusations. But they very calmly asked her if she wished to walk out to the car or if they had to restrain her and carry her out. This was after she had given her partner quite a severe beating with a weapon, so I do quite admire how they manage to keep their cool.

It has to be difficult assessing the situation when they go out to a report, my experience is that female perpetrators are great actors as they can put on this front as though they haven't done anything or the opposite and turn on the tears to put the focus of the police attention on the victim. Again, this is why the terminology "gendered crime" should not be used, as it can alter their perspective on the incident in front of them.

But it is worth reporting these incidents to the police as even if you do not wish to press charges, there is a record then that is held and can potentially help to build a case in the future if a time arises that you do wish to take things further. A word of caution though, there are some things that you may report but not want to go further but the police do have the authority to press charges without your consent if they feel they need to.

So, what can you as a male victim expect from the police should you need to call them out? Quite simply, the exact same treatment that a female victim would receive. You should expect them to:

- Respond quickly to your call for help.
- They should always speak to you and your partner separately so as they can gain a good understanding of what has occurred.
- Take a statement from you and any other witnesses to thoroughly investigate the incident.
- They should collect evidence, things like weapons that were used and pictures of damage to any property or injuries that you may have received.
- Most importantly, they should ensure that you (and any children that you have) are safe. That means they should arrest the perpetrator or remove them from the property (in the UK by using an order at their disposal that we will cover in the next chapter). They may also consider removing you from the property (again with children if you have them) if they feel that would be a safer option.
- They should also always give you details of where you can get support, give you a crime reference number and keep you updated on any developments.

If you are ever in the position that this does not happen, do not be afraid to complain as it is only by doing this that we can change the small minority of times that this does happen.

IDVA and ISVA

I know what you're thinking, what the hell are these? Here in the UK, IDVA stands for Independent Domestic Violence Advisors and ISVA for Independent Sexual Violence

Advisors. They obviously have very specific roles to do with victims of domestic abuse.

IDVA's main role is to address the safety of the victims and their dependents in high-risk cases. They do not just focus on the short-term safety but work with the victims over their long-term safety plans (over three months). They will also become the victim's single point of contact and will help to guide them through the criminal justice process. There is plenty of evidence in the UK that backs up the fact that when there is IDVA involvement, there is a clear improvement in the victim's safety. I myself know a few IDVAs (including Josh, who I work with at Break the Silence UK) and have seen the work they do; it is an amazing resource to have.

ISVA's provide specialist support to victims and survivors of sexual violence and abuse irrespective of whether they have reported it to the police or not. They can provide the victims and survivors with information on the criminal justice process (just like IDVAs can) and can also attend interviews and court appearances with the victims. ISVAs can also provide information on health services and again, attend with the victims if they want them to. Most importantly though, they are there to listen to the experiences of their clients and provide the emotional support they need whilst addressing what has happened to them.

Most UK based domestic abuse services have these attached to them but it can be different depending where you live within the country. Your best bet is to research it via an internet search engine, as there are details of services in many different countries to be found.

Multi-Agency Risk Assessment Conference or MARAC

One last resource that is available when it comes to keeping safe in the UK, and involves both the police and IDVAs, is MARAC. A Multi-Agency Risk Assessment Conference is a regular meeting within your area where they discuss how to keep high-risk victims safe from harm. I do know a lot about these conferences as I myself have been to many to represent victims of abuse. For the ones that I attended, there would be police, IDVA, children's services, health services, housing workers and anyone else that was relevant to the case all sat together to talk about the victim, their family and the perpetrator. The aims of MARAC are quite simple:

- To share information between agencies in order to increase the safety and wellbeing of the victims and their families.
- To determine if the perpetrator poses a significant risk of harm.
- To work on a multi-agency action and risk management plan to support all those that are at risk. This works well because everyone knows their role and they all work together to achieve set outcomes. This process also improves agencies' accountability in cases of abuse.
- They also aim to reduce the amount of repeat victimisation.

Believe me, they are very good at what they do. I have seen victims moved within days following a MARAC as they were deemed to be too high-risk to remain where they were. Their effectiveness has been evidenced as across the country, 42% of victims experienced no repeat incidents following MARAC, that's nearly half of all the cases heard. But for those that did suffer repeat victimisation, they typically called the police a lot earlier than they would have before, so again a reduction in harm. Equally as important is that the number of children that were referred to children's services for extra support through MARAC has risen from 5% to 50% and as we looked at earlier domestic abuse does affect children in a big way.

My final words in this section are about moving forwards with your life, learn from what you have experienced and know the warning signs to watch for. Behaviours and tactics that we have looked at and discussed throughout this book stay with you. If you experience them again in the future, you will know, you'll get that gut instinct. Trust your gut instinct, if something doesn't feel right then it probably isn't right. Gut instinct is based on experiences in the past, listen to it. Secondly, look out for someone always looking to blame and not taking responsibility for their own actions. Finally, being aware of someone over contacting you, you know what I mean when they send you a text followed by one 5 minutes later saying "why haven't you text me back". I could go on forever but these three came from a group of male victims that I worked with so I wanted to share them with you.

So, there we have it, that's my chapter around safety and keeping safe. As you can see there is plenty that can be done and plenty of people that can support you when it comes to keeping safe in domestic abuse situations regardless of where in the world you live. Safety plans are safety plans, no matter where you are, the only difference is the services available to victims in their area.

Chapter Fourteen
Just What Are Your
Legal Options?

For this chapter, we will be looking at what is available in the UK in terms of legal options. The range of protective measures available each country will differ and to write about them all would be a book in itself. However, some of what we cover here may help you get an understanding and give you an idea of what to look for if based in any other country.

Criminal Law

In the last chapter, we discussed about what you should expect to receive from the police compared to some of the experiences some males I have supported have received and some of the other services that can help keep you safe as a victim of domestic abuse. Sadly though, on the whole, the reports I have read from male victims show that they haven't been treated in the way they should have and this is something that has to change. Maybe it is because of these negative experiences that it is estimated that less than half of all incidents of domestic abuse actually get reported to the police, some would even go further than that and estimate that it could be as low as a third. The fact remains that for criminal law to be able to protect victims of abuse, the victim does need to show tremendous strength and report their suffering to the police. If this is done, then there are a whole range of charges that can be brought against the perpetrator if there is enough evidence.

Strangely, even though the number of estimated victims is well into the millions, there is no single crime of domestic abuse; it is actually made up of a number of other offences such as:

- Common assault
- Assault occasioning actual bodily harm (ABH)
- Unlawful wounding or inflicting grievous bodily harm (GBH)
- Threats to kill
- Kidnapping
- Attempted murder
- Murder
- A range of sexual assaults

So, it does beg the question, just how any people are actually charged and sentenced with domestic abuse offences if it is these types of offences they are charged with.

The other offence that someone can now be charged with is that of coercive and controlling behaviour against an intimate partner or family member. This is a relative newbie in terms of law as it only came into effect on 29th December 2015. It was recognised that the fear of abuse that domestic abuse victims suffer within that toxic relationship wasn't actually covered by any other offence.

Now to explain in more detail as to how someone is found guilty under this law. A person has committed an offence if:

- Person A (the perpetrator) repeatedly or continuously engages in behaviours towards Person B (the victim) that is controlling or coercive.
- At the time of the behaviour, Person A (the perpetrator) was personally connected to Person B (the victim). They are considered personally connected if they are in an intimate personal relationship, if they live together or are family members who live together, or if they have previously been in an intimate relationship.
- The behaviour has a serious effect on Person B (the victim)
- Person A (the perpetrator) knows, or ought to know, that the behaviour will have a serious effect on Person B (the victim).

There are two ways in which, under this law, it can be proven that the perpetrator's behaviour has a serious effect on their victim and these are:

- If it causes the victim fear that violence will be used against them on at least two separate occasions.
- If it causes the victim serious alarm or distress which has a detrimental effect on their ability to complete day-to-day activities.

There are many behaviours that a perpetrator could use against their victim which we have covered within these pages that could and would be considered behaviours that factor into this law. The good news is that when this law is applied correctly and a perpetrator is found guilty of this offence, they can face a maximum sentence of five years imprisonment or a fine, in some cases they may get both. I have had people say to me, and not just victims, "Five years? Is that it for what they have done?" I have my own personal views on this but this is what the law states and I'm not in a position to change this.

When it comes to criminal law, it is not down to the victim to decide if charges should be brought against the perpetrator, they also don't have the ability to withdraw charges. The decision in both of these lies with the police and with the Crown Prosecution Service (CPS) and is based on the evidence that is collected and presented to them. If there is sufficient evidence to provide a realistic prospect of conviction, they will make a decision to charge.

What we do have in some areas of the UK now, which we are very lucky to have, are SDVC's, or to use their correct titles, Specialist Domestic Violence Courts, who do exactly what their name suggests. They have been designed to bring together all the various services that can support the victims through the whole court process. We are talking IDVAs, police, probation, adult or child services, housing, the CPS, the list could go on and on. The aim of doing this is to ensure that the victim has the best chance of bringing their perpetrator to justice through the criminal law route. There has been the implementation of special measures within these courts too with the addition of screens, video links so as the victim can be in a separate room, court escorts and seating away from the perpetrator to help the victim through this process.

The police do have a few other options that they can seek to use in the form of Domestic Violence Protection Orders (DVPOs) and Domestic Violence Protection Notices (DVPNs). These were rolled out as new measures that all police forces could take in 2014. They are civil orders that allow police and magistrates to provide victims with protective measures immediately after an incident of domestic abuse where there is insufficient evidence for them to charge a perpetrator. The Domestic Violence Protection Notices are effectively emergency non-molestation orders and eviction notices that they can use when attending an incident. This notice effectively removes the perpetrator from the property for 48 hours which then allows the police to make an application to the magistrate for a Domestic Violence Protection Order which can prevent the perpetrator returning to the home or having any contact what-so-ever with the victim for a further 28 days. These orders can be effective as they give the victim a little breathing space to seek help and assistance.

Can a perpetrator breach these orders, you ask? As with any orders, yes, they can but to do so can result in a two-month custodial sentence or a fine up to £5,000.

Civil Law

Alongside the protection offered by criminal law, victims may also want to look at what options are open to them under civil law. These options come under the Family Law Act of

1996, Part IV, which provides protection from physical, psychological, emotional and sexual abuse in the form of civil orders. These orders place legal restrictions on perpetrators of domestic abuse in an attempt to try and prevent further abuse to the victims. In most cases, these orders will last for about 6 months but in some situations, they will be extended for longer periods of time. The two civil orders that would normally be considered are:

- Non-molestation order (usually lasts for one year)
- Occupation order (usually lasts for six months but can get a further six months' extension)

So, what are they exactly? Let me take you through them and explain.

Non-Molestation Order

The non-molestation order stops the perpetrator from exposing their victim to certain behaviours. These are behaviours like using or threatening violence, using intimidation, harassment or pestering either directly from the perpetrator or indirectly through other people. These orders can also cover the victim's children and can have specific restrictions attached such as no telephone or email contact. They can also be used to prevent a perpetrator from entering a certain area, usually around the home, school or work of those the order is there to protect. These orders can be done in a DIY way by using court form FL401. Victims can also call the courts for an appointment to apply "ex-parte" which means without notice to the perpetrator. By law, all family courts should have slots for emergency appointments and once granted, the order can be served on the perpetrator without the chance to contest.

The non-molestation order is an arrest-able offence if it is breached by the perpetrator.

Occupation Order

Occupation orders regulate victims and perpetrators' rights regarding their home address. The order makes a decision on who can live in, and visits, the family home and can also be used to restrict the perpetrator from the surrounding areas.

Occupation orders can be granted with an attached power of arrest if the perpetrator decides to breach the restrictions put in place.

Both of these orders, the non-molestation order and the occupation order are intended to secure future protection for victims of abuse. However, it is important to remember that any order applied for is at the discretion of the judge presiding over the court and there is no guarantee that an application will be successful. As with the non-molestation order, a victim can apply directly to the court by completing court form fl401 (which is also available online) and at present there is no fee payable for applying for it.

As with all things, there are both positives and negatives to them and the civil law option is no different. On the plus side, it gives further options to victims of domestic abuse to secure their safety and they do offer penalties if they are breached. But on the negative side, there has been a reduction in the funding available to access these orders if the victim is not confident in applying for it themselves, meaning in most cases, victims can be left liable to pay legal fees to their chosen solicitor. There is also very little evidence out there into just how effective these orders actually are, part of this is also dependent on if the police are acting on the breaches to these orders. I have heard one story that as much as I have tried to confirm it, I have been unable to, that alleges a breach of a non-molestation order was met with a £20 fine for the perpetrator. If this is true, what sort of a message is this sending out?

When it comes to civil law, victims of domestic abuse can access assistance through the National Centre for Domestic Violence (NCDV) in obtaining these orders from their local county courts. This service is completely free and they can usually get an emergency injunction in place within 24 hours of your first contact with them. They do this in three stages, which are:

1. They assess if you are eligible for an emergency injunction – they have to ensure that you and the perpetrator are "associated" in the eyes of the law and that there has been a recent use or threat of violence within the last 10 days (this is a criterion for an emergency injunction).

2. They will then identify the best course of action for your case – if you are eligible for legal aid, they will work alongside a firm of solicitors, but if not, they will aim to put you in contact with a McKenzie friend from within your area. McKenzie friends are experienced case workers who can help prepare your application and assist you in court.

3. A case worker will make contact with you to prepare the injunction application – this is usually done over the phone as the need to prepare a statement that sets out why the injunction is needed. If the victim has been recording incidents via the Bright Sky app mentioned earlier, this will provide the evidence. Once they have done this, they will arrange a time for you to go to court. If the court does grant the order applied for, they will then help the victim to serve the order to the perpetrator.

This is an incredibly valuable service that the NCDV offer to support victims of abuse. You can contact the NCDV for support on **0800 970 2070** or by texting NCDV to **60777** and they will call you back. They also have the ability to make a referral for an injunction directly on their main website page which is www.ncdv.org.uk.

Clare's Law

The Domestic Violence Disclosure Scheme or Clare's Law as it is more commonly known (after the case that led to its creation) gives any member of the public the right to ask the police if their partner may pose a risk to them. Under this law, members of the public can also make enquiries into the partner of a close friend or family member. The case that I'm talking about that led to the creation of this law is that of Clare Wood, a 36-year-old woman who was strangled and then her body set on fire by her ex-boyfriend in February 2009. He had a record of violence towards women.

For anyone to make an application under Clare's Law, all they would need to do is attend any police station where a member of staff will take details of what prompted the enquiry and talk you through what the process is. What needs to be remembered here is that if it is apparent a crime has been committed, the police do need to act on that information.

Once an application has been received, the police will carry out a range of checks and if these reveal a record of abusive offences or suggest a risk of violence, they then consider sharing the information. If they do decide to make a disclosure, this is usually done directly to the person who is at risk as the aim of the scheme is to help people make more informed decisions on continuing the relationship and to provide help and support when making that choice. The person making the actual application may actually receive no notification of any aspect of the decision or disclosure.

Again, this is a really valuable scheme that can make a real difference when tackling domestic abuse.

Child Contact

When we were looking at child contact within the behaviours used to perpetrate domestic abuse, I said that as part of the legal options, I would talk you through how to apply for contact with your own children through the courts. Sadly, it is a massive tactic that perpetrators use against their male victims and is something that I have come across just too many times and it is heart-breaking.

One of the most common talking points with the men that I shared these experiences with was that they had taken the free legal advice and that solicitors could charge anywhere between £120 to £200 per hour and having attended the family courts before that could easily be £600 for one court session, not taking into account all the form filling, letters and general paperwork that they do. In a straight forward, easy case where all parties agree, it could cost anywhere from £3000 plus. When you're talking about an abusive relationship and all that brings with it, it could be substantially more.

The alternative is that you could make an application directly to the court yourself and have a friend or family member to support you. It is a much cheaper option that is available but obviously you then don't get the professional advice of a solicitor. To apply directly to the court, you would need to compete the form C100 that can be obtained online by simply putting C100 into your search engine. You will see that the form in itself is very easy to complete and there are also additional forms that you can complete being a victim of domestic abuse. The C1a is for allegations of harm and domestic violence where you can give details of the abuse to the judge so they are aware of what you as the victim have suffered or concerns of abuse around the children. My advice to you around this is use the information that you have been recording, things that can be evidenced. You may also choose to complete the C8 form which keeps your contact details private from the other party, which again is a massive tool that can be used to protect yourself as the victim of abuse.

So, the big question, I know you're sat there thinking, "This is all well and good but how much does this cost?" The answer is currently £215, which granted isn't a small amount of money but compared to the cost that can be accrued through solicitors, it's actually pretty amazing!

Once the application has been submitted and the fee paid, the court will arrange what is known as a "directions hearing" with both parents present. Usually, these meetings will be attended by a family court advisor from the Children and Family Court Advisory and Support Service (CAFCASS). The aim of this "directions hearing" is for the judge or magistrate to try and work out:

- What you can agree.
- What you can't agree.
- If your child is at risk in any way (which is why the C1a form around domestic abuse is important).

They will try to encourage both parents to come to an agreement in the child's best interests, which when it comes to cases of domestic abuse, is very unlikely to happen. As we looked at earlier, children are used effectively as a great weapon by perpetrators against their victims and to back down is seen as relinquishing a level of power and control. You will probably find that there are a number of issues and obstacles placed in the way, as well as a level of false accusations aimed at you.

If it is the likely case that an agreement cannot be reached, the judge or magistrate will set out a timetable for what needs to happen next. It may be that they suggest meeting with a mediator to try and reach an agreement which I would always argue against in cases where domestic abuse is involved. But regardless of what they ask the parents to do, they will also ask the CAFCASS official to provide a report to them on the case to help decide what is best for the child. It is part of the usual process that the CAFCASS officer will ask your child about their feelings and what they want, but don't worry, this is not done in the presence of the mother (in the case of male victims).

When making a decision around what is best for the children, the judge or magistrate will always put the child's welfare first. This is not something they take lightly and do take all the information presented into consideration when reaching a decision. Just to give an example of some of the things they think about, here are just a few:

- What the child's own wishes are and their feelings.
- The child's physical, emotional and educational needs and the ability of the parents to meet these needs.
- The effects of any changes on the child and any possible risks of harm to the child.

Ultimately, the judge or magistrate will only make an order if they think it is in the best interest of the child.

In terms of the types of contact, certainly that can depend on how long it has been since there has been any contact with the child or if the judge or magistrate deems there is any potential risk to the child (risk of the non-resident parent fleeing with the child). My experience whilst working within the domestic abuse service when it came to child contact for non-resident parents generally followed a similar pattern. Generally, contact would start within a contact centre where the sessions were supervised by a member of staff for 6 to 8 sessions where the member of staff remains present throughout, making notes on how the session went and any concerns before moving on to having supported contact where again a neutral member of staff is there but not monitoring the session as closely. If these go well, it can then be explored for someone else to support the contact out in the community. This could be a grandparent, another relative or a mutual friend if this can be agreed and allows a little more freedom on what can be done. It would be hoped as part of the progression of the contact that this could then follow up to unsupervised contact with your child. In some cases, that does happen and it should as it is equally important for a child to spend time with both their parents.

Unfortunately, I have also experienced the process manipulated by the perpetrator and the whole process fall apart. As I already went in to in the chapter about children, there was the case where the perpetrator would not agree on anyone local that she was related to or my client was related to for supported contact in the community after what was an excellent first 8 sessions of supervised contact with no concerns. The only people she would agree to were the victim's parents who lived over 200 miles away and were both elderly. Of course, they both agreed to it as they wanted to see their grandchild and wanted to support their son having contact with his child. I had my reservations as did my client, which is exactly what happened as being elderly, when they were ill, they were unable to travel which stopped contact and the blame laid at the feet of the victim meaning the process had to start again.

On another occasion, I experienced a rather hostile atmosphere in the waiting area from the perpetrator and a male friend that were at the court for the contact hearing with comments and intimidating postures and looks aimed at us.

But there are separate waiting areas that can be accessed so don't be afraid to ask.

What has moved these types of cases on a lot is that there has been a great deal of training for magistrates around domestic abuse and that for cases they may be dealing with, it could be equally as likely that it is the father that is suffering abuse as it is the mother. As a result of this, it is my belief that male victims that are trying to gain contact with their children are being given more of a fair chance at making this happen.

Chapter Fifteen
Identifying What is a
Healthy Relationship

As I said right back at the start of the book within the foreword, experience has taught me that for so many men that are locked within abusive relationships, they do not know that the behaviours their partner is showing them are in fact abusive. Furthermore, they don't seem to know what is and isn't acceptable behaviour from their partner and that is also an issue. For that reason alone, I decided that a big part of this journey would be to look at what a healthy relationship actually is. Being able to truly understand what this is can help you to step back and analyse the behaviours that you may be facing from your partner. This also works for families and friends when they are looking at the behaviours that they have been privy to with loved ones that they have concerns about.

So here we go then, just what is a healthy relationship? Is there an easy answer to this question? Regardless of where you look for the answer, the concept of a healthy relationship is the same. It is a relationship that strives to see that both partners feel the support of the other whilst still being able to maintain their own independence. I agree with this viewpoint entirely and the keyword in all this is the word "support". For any relationship to be truly healthy there are three essential ingredients with a sprinkling of others. The three essential components will be trust, respect and support. Without these fundamentals, a relationship cannot on any level be considered healthy.

If these ingredients are there, your partner will encourage you to have outside interests that you pursue, this could be a hobby that you are interested in or it could be around personal development if you wanted to look more at further education. My wife has done this for me. Not only does she support me with the work Break the Silence UK does, but also supports me with studying for my Masters in Understanding Domestic and Sexual Violence. This is a massive thing for me, as it allows me to develop the understanding that I have further in a subject I am passionate about. My wife also supported and encouraged me to develop other ways I could help people, by studying in my spare time to complete my CBT diploma and NLP qualification, my first qualifications since leaving school over 20 years ago.

In a healthy relationship, your partner would also always be welcoming to your family and friends. Why? Because they are important to you, and therefore, important to them. In our relationships, we support each other but we also get the love and support from those that extend out from the relationship in the form of our families and friends.

Other important components that make a healthy relationship are skills like communication. Is it possible to have any type of relationship with another person if there is no communication, let alone a healthy one? Certainly, within a healthy relationship, you will find that the couple will listen to one another, allowing each other the time to talk and respond. They will give the other the opportunity to express their views and to talk freely and openly about their emotions and how they feel. You cannot read your partner's mind and they cannot read yours, being able to talk in this way leads to honesty and mutual respect.

They will still make criticisms, everyone does in some way but if the relationship is healthy, this will be done in a constructive way that is designed to help, to build them up and encourage them to try again and not in a way to put them down and question their abilities. Constructive criticism focuses on both the positive and negative aspects of what has been done and working in partnership to look for other possible solutions. Part of good communication is being able to openly discuss and recognise the need for change and be open to compromise. Compromise requires honesty, trust and support to create an agreement that is acceptable to both partners. It's about being happy to give a little to make those changes and each takes responsibility for their own actions.

Looking at all the above always remind me of what I myself was once told, that I would like to share. When two people enter a relationship, each of them has their own views on how the relationship should be. Do these views always match? Probably never, and without communication how can we find that happy medium? Communication and compromise are key to achieving this.

Healthy partners will always be consistent with one another and they will know what to expect. We do have bad days; everyone does, but by also being honest and open at all times, this can be addressed. If we make a mistake then that is okay, we all make mistakes, every one of us and people learn from their mistakes. Within a healthy relationship, your partner certainly won't judge you for making a mistake. They will enable you to be able to admit that you have done something wrong, claim responsibility for your action and be able to move on building the relationship, not have to live with fear. We all have different opinions when it comes to different things and in a healthy relationship, this is good because both parties have a mutual respect for each other's opinions and even if they do not agree with their point of view, they make an effort to understand it and be mindful of where they are coming from.

Our partners respect us for who we are, we are the person they fell in love with and they also respect our physical appearance, warts and all! Yes, over the years we may put on a few pounds but they see our positive qualities and don't put us down over it. Both partners do show each other physical affection on a regular basis, whether it is holding hands walking to the shops or whilst watching television or a quick hug and kiss when one of them returns home from work. One thing they do not do, though, is treat each other as objects or possessions.

In healthy relationships, the partners are happy to discuss all aspects of their physical relationship in an open and honest way. It could be that their partner has started doing something or suggested trying something that makes them feel uncomfortable or causes them pain. But this doesn't develop into a massive issue as they feel confident and happy that they can openly discuss this with their partner without it becoming uncomfortable. When it comes to sex, they are happy at any time for their partner to say no, this is absolutely fine as it quite rightly should be without trying to force the issue.

Shared responsibilities are important for any healthy relationship, whether it's through agreed compromises or through honest discussions for things like household duties and bills. It's about the inclusion of both parties in making the decisions that need to be made and not just making those decisions independently of each other or being dictated to. For those that are parents, it's about both equally supporting and encouraging the children in all aspects of their lives and any possible discussions that need to be held are done together and in total support. Just recently in our home, we needed to have a discussion about internet safety and were both saying the same thing, not making our daughter feel scared but making her feel comfortable to come and speak to us about anything that she is concerned about. But it's also about parents being able to acknowledge when they are not right and admitting this and apologising to their children.

So, do we believe this is achievable? Is there actually a relationship out there that can be described as perfectly healthy? In my experience, yes, this can be achieved. Like all things though it does take work, but when both partners are working towards the same goal, it can be achieved. People have also asked the question, "can those that have been victims of abuse really ever experience a healthy relationship?" The answer is, undoubtedly, yes. I myself have experienced an abusive relationship in the past but would consider the relationship between myself and my wife to be extremely healthy. I also know of more than a handful of male victims of abuse that have gone on from really abusive relationships to have happy healthy relationships.

Another way to look at this is the equality wheel; this is much like the power and control wheel but looking at what makes a healthy relationship. This was a concept also created by the Minnesota Domestic Abuse Intervention Project (can be viewed online) as a reference point for female victims that couldn't identify with what a healthy relationship looked like. As with the alternative version of the power and control wheel, the example text I have chosen to show you has been changed to be gender neutral as equality applies to anyone. See for yourself…

- **Open Communication** – being able to express your feelings and opinions, knowing it's OK to disagree, saying what you mean and meaning what you say.
- **Intimacy** – respecting your partner's boundaries, respecting each other's privacy, not pressuring, being faithful.
- **Physical Affection** – holding hands, hugging, kissing, sitting or standing with your arm on your partner's shoulder, respecting each other's right to say no, asking before acting.
- **Fairness and Negotiation** – accepting change, being willing to compromise, working to find solutions that are agreeable to both people, agreeing to disagree sometimes.
- **Shared Responsibility** – making decisions together, splitting or alternating the costs on dates, doing things for each other, going places you both enjoy, giving as much as you receive.
- **Respect** – paying attention to your partner even when friends are around, valuing your partners opinion even if it differs from yours, listen to what your partner has to say.

- **Trust and Support** – being supportive, wanting the best for your partner, knowing what your partner likes, offering encouragement when necessary, being OK with your partner having different friends.
- **Honesty and Responsibility** – not making excuses for your partner's or for your own actions, admitting when you are wrong, keeping your word, not cancelling plans.

Do you see? Gender is not a factor when it comes to equality. I think that to look at this is a reference point or to get an overview of what an equal and healthy relationship is. It sums it up in an easy-to-understand way.

But when it comes down to being an equal in a relationship, you can still only take responsibility for your behaviours. We all have certain basic rights in our lives, they are not selfish in any way, shape or form (although some would disagree with that) and they belong to everyone. They belong to you, they belong to your partner, they belong to your children, they belong to your neighbour, and they even belong to Joe Bloggs down the street. They belong to EVERYONE. Acceptance of these rights must come first and foremost if someone wants to move on from surviving with the old patterns of life in abuse to a new way of taking back control of your life. This has got you intrigued as to what these rights are, hasn't it?

Let me share them with you.

1. You have the right to be you, the real you and you have the right to put yourself first.
2. You have the right to feel and to be safe.

3. You have the right to love, to be loved and treated with respect that you deserve.
4. You have the right to make mistakes, we are all human, not perfect.
5. You have the right to your own privacy.
6. You have the right to have your own opinions, to be able to express them freely and for those opinions to be taken seriously.
7. You have the right to be angry, to express your feeling and say something if you are treated unfairly or abusively by anyone.
8. You have a right to earn your own income and to control that income in whatever way you see fit.
9. You have the right to develop, to grow both personally and professionally.
10. You have the right to change, change your thoughts, feelings and to change your mind.
11. You have the right to say no.
12. You have the right to ask questions about anything that affects your life.
13. You have the right to be in control of your own life and if you are not happy with it, to change it as you see fit.

What do you think reading this? Do you think these basic rights of life can be achieved by everyone and still be part of a healthy relationship? I believe that they can as these basic principles go hand in hand with a healthy relationship as if you have a partner that truly respects you, then these can easily be achieved.

Let me end this section with a quote I once had shared with me, "Unresolved conflict is like rust, you cannot leave it and hope it just goes away. If conflict is dealt with properly in a respectful way, it can make a relationship stronger and more trusting."

Chapter Sixteen
Information for Relatives

It's hard, isn't it? When that son or brother suddenly disappears and you have no idea what has happened to them. When you get the abusive text messages from their number and just can't believe that it could be them behind it.

There will be many of you out there who know the feelings I'm speaking of, as it is hard and very upsetting for a parent or any family member to think, or in some cases know, that someone is hurting a person you love. As a parent, a mother or father, your first thought will probably be to protect that person and put a stop to this behaviour, but the fact is that it isn't always possible and it can drive them further away. To intervene can be extremely dangerous, maybe not to you but more likely to your loved one, but to ignore is just as dangerous.

So, what can you do? Firstly, try to understand what it is he is experiencing, obviously you don't know all the ins and outs of what he is being subjected to, but I hope that I can give you a little bit of an insight through this book.

Anybody that is suffering from domestic abuse will be often overwhelmed by fear. Mainly a fear of the unknown as they know something will happen, just not what or when. This fear can impact his every decision, knowing that one wrong move could lead to violence. If there are children in the relationship as well, I can assure you he will be feeling a fear over their safety and what could happen to them. We should never underestimate what fear can do to a person. This fear will leave them living in fight, flight or freeze mode constantly, with no moments of relief.

As you will have read earlier on, the perpetrator of the abuse is very convincing in what they say and on deflecting the blame for any abuse back on their victim, blaming things that they may have done for what is happening. Over a period of time, victims of abuse can come to believe that maybe they are partially to blame and if they change the way they are maybe the abuse will stop. Sadly, evidence says that this is hardly ever the case and that the abuse will continue to get worse. By the time a victim has got to this stage within the relationship, they may feel resigned to their fate so to speak, they may not see that they have a future let alone make any decisions about it.

I have also spoken a few times about the war that is going on in the mind of the victim, as he still loves his partner but wishes the abuse would stop. Certainly, for many of the men that I have worked with, they lived at some point in the constant hope that this is just a rough patch and the days when things were good will soon return. Again, sadly this will not happen as most of them realised.

Most of all, a male victim will be feeling shame and embarrassment over what has happened to them. It is society that has a lot to answer for on that. We have just entered 2021 and still some in society believe that male victims are weak and in some way a bit of a joke, as they can't defend themselves. This may be why so many women are getting away in this kind of abuse to men, the fear of being rejected by society.

Now you have a little bit of an insight into some of the things that may be happening for them, through what you have read so far, it's time to look at what you can do to help.

Talk to them, to try and help them open up to you. One of the biggest thing's men used to say to me is that they wished someone had just asked "are you ok?" They may not have answered but at least they would have known someone was there. Maybe start by letting them know that you are worried or concerned about them and their well-being. You may have to try this several times before they start to open up, as evidence show that there will be over 30 incidents of abuse before someone will contemplate looking for help. It's about persistence, not in pushing them, but letting them know you are there.

What you will need to do once he is ready to open up, is to ensure that you listen to what he tells you and no matter how far-fetched some of the things he may say seem, believe it, as it is probably true. Taking all of this in and not judging him are key, put all of your focus on supporting him and trying to reclaim some of his previous confidence.

What is really important for you try and do is, despite what your instincts are telling you to say, don't tell him he has to leave. Although that may be what you really want him to do you have to realise that some men just aren't ready to leave through fear and other things, and if they do say that they are staying, the worst thing you can do is criticise their decision as it will just put a barrier between you. If you are lucky enough to still have contact, that in itself is massive, as isolation is one of the biggest tactics used against men, keeping them from becoming isolated and wholly dependent on their partner is important. It would not be a bad idea to ensure that you are encouraging them to keep on doing things they enjoy, as that could keep them from becoming isolated also.

One important thing that you could offer to do for him, is to hold on to his survivor pack as then he will know that it is safe, and also offer to be the person he calls when he is in danger. This will mean agreeing a code word that can be used in times of need when he can't call for help himself.

Above anything else though, be patient. This most likely is something that will not be resolved overnight. This can prove frustrating and you may start to make plans yourself, but this will only put barriers between you. He needs to be able to make the decisions himself, as it is not something he will have been able to do in the relationship, as all power and control will have been taken from him. It can take time to fully recognise and understand the extent of the abuse they have been suffering. This is the very first step and is one that they need to take on their own.

References

Predominantly the material held within this book has come from my own knowledge and experiences. I have, however, used a few other places as reference points when putting the content together; these are:

- Rejuvenate Programme – support programme for male victims of domestic abuse
- Mankind Initiative – facts and figures from Mankind Initiative statistics and advertising campaigns
- Men's Advice Line – Confirmation on Orders and other agencies